TEACH US

TO

PRAY

TEACH US TO PRAY

What We Can Learn from Scripture

―――――――――◦―――――――――

CARLA D. SUNBERG

𝍫

THE FOUNDRY
PUBLISHING®

Copyright © 2023 by Carla D. Sunberg
The Foundry Publishing®
PO Box 419527
Kansas City, MO 64141
thefoundrypublishing.com

978-0-8341-4178-0

Cover design: Rob Monacelli
Interior design: Sharon Page

Library of Congress Cataloging-in-Publication Data
A complete catalog record for this book is available from the Library of Congress.

The internet addresses, email addresses, and phone numbers in this book are accurate at the time of publication. They are provided as a resource. The Foundry Publishing does not endorse them or vouch for their content or permanence.

TABLE OF CONTENTS

Introduction   7

1. Why Pray?   11

2. Jesus Teaches Us to Pray   21

3. Prayer and Participation in the Mission   37

4. Posture in Prayer   53

5. Practicing What We've Been Taught   65

6. Mentoring Young Leaders:
   Praying with Paul and Timothy   77

7. Prayer as Foundational to Spiritual Growth:
   Paul and the Ephesians   91

8. The Necessity of Prayer   101

9. Pragmatic Prayers   115

10. Prayer in the Psalms   125

Closing Thoughts   139

INTRODUCTION

I used to watch my grandfather in awe. Several times a day he would enter a time of devotion and prayer. Long passages of psalms he had memorized floated from his lips as though they were his own words. In a smooth transition, the words from Scripture became words of prayer, and my grandfather appeared to be swept away in a private and intimate conversation with the Lord. Somehow it felt as if I were an interloper, peering into something that was happening on holy ground. My father referred to his own father's faith as "mystical"—something that was not describable because we all recognized a depth of relationship that was beyond the earthly. His prayer life revealed a genuine relationship that reflected the reality of God. If you had any doubt as to the existence of God, all you had to do was listen to Grandpa's prayers. Grandpa Johnson knew how to pray, and from a young age this truth tugged at my heart. I wanted to know Jesus the way Grandpa knew Jesus.

I find that people often take prayer for granted. I have sat in numerous meetings with leaders discussing prayer.

Once, on the mission field, we talked about putting a specific emphasis on prayer in a strategic document. Someone responded, "Oh, that's a given." But then I thought that I'm not sure it is. Maybe in my grandfather's time, it was a given that Christians knew prayer should encompass every part of our lives and certainly every aspect of ministry. It seems the past generations may have failed to pass on the spiritual gift of prayer to a new generation.

A number of years ago I was in the United Kingdom, sitting in a series of all-day lectures on Wesleyanism. One presenter was speaking about a second wave of Wesleyan influence in England that was somewhat related to the Holiness camp meetings in the United States near the end of the nineteenth and beginning of the twentieth centuries. The presenter read a letter from someone who had attended the camp meeting in the United States, and I found it fascinating. The individual outlined the schedule for the day, which began with an early-morning prayer meeting. They broke for breakfast, then returned to the tent or tabernacle for another session of prayer. Evidently, this was a time when many would come forward to the "mourner's bench" and cry out for God's Spirit to be poured out upon the gathering. This would go on for an hour or two. The witness said the presence of the Spirit of God was so "thick" that people were giving their lives to Christ over the lunch hour. Again, in the afternoon, the people gathered, some around the mourner's bench, others pacing the aisles as they prayed and interceded for the needs of the world and of God's people. Eventually there was an evening service in which the Word was preached, and the altars were lined with those seeking a deeper walk with Christ. The author of the letter warned that there should not be too much preaching, for it could overshadow the great need for prayer. This letter, written more than a hundred years ago, made an impression on me and made me want to know more about prayer.

Sadly, it seems that these protracted periods of time spent in prayer are now part of history for the majority of Christians. Somehow prayer is a spiritual discipline that has not been passed on through the generations. In a recent meeting on discipleship, we spoke of the importance of prayer only to discover that we had never defined prayer and that, for many new believers, the concept was simply foreign. Nothing can be taken for granted. If we are going to be disciples of Jesus Christ, then we must be people of prayer.

A number of years ago I read a book called *The Divine Mentor* that encourages us to find mentors in the Word of God. My grandfather is no longer living, and there are times I wish I could sit under his mentorship and learn to pray the way he did. All the previous generations in my family have now passed on, so I have looked to Scripture to provide me with mentors who can teach me to pray. I confess I have been hesitant to write this book because I still have much more to learn about prayer, but I do know I have learned a great deal from what I have gleaned in the Word of God. I invite you to join me in this journey of mentorship, where we allow Scripture to pour into our lives and teach us, a new generation, to be people of prayer.

1
WHY PRAY?

———○———

Finally, be strong in the Lord and in his mighty power. Put on the full armor of God, so that you can take your stand against the devil's schemes. For our struggle is not against flesh and blood, but against the rulers, against the authorities, against the powers of this dark world and against the spiritual forces of evil in the heavenly realms. Therefore put on the full armor of God, so that when the day of evil comes, you may be able to stand your ground, and after you have done everything, to stand. Stand firm then, with the belt of truth buckled around your waist, with the breastplate of righteousness in place, and with your feet fitted with the readiness that comes from the gospel of peace. In addition to all this, take up the shield of faith, with which you can extinguish all the flaming arrows of the evil one. Take the helmet of salvation and the sword of the Spirit, which is the word of God.

—Ephesians 6:10–17

The church in Ephesus was filled with followers of Christ who were growing and developing in their discipleship. The city itself was a cosmopolitan center where people from around the known world came to visit the temple of the Greek goddess Artemis (or the Roman version, Diana). The temple to this goddess was an incredible building, one of the seven wonders of the ancient world. The secular world, filled as it was with pagan worship, encroached upon the fledgling spiritual lives of the new believers. Standing firm in their faith was becoming a significant challenge. Therefore, Paul wanted to instruct them on the ways in which they could stand firm, beginning by putting on the full armor of God, which has a lot to do with prayer.

There are many pieces to the armor of God as described by Paul, but overall, the purpose is to be strong in the Lord and in the Lord's power. The armor reflects the power of Jesus in our lives, which gives us the ability to withstand the devil. Far too often we fail to realize there are ongoing battles in the heavenly realms, but Paul wanted to provide the church with a vision of warfare between good and evil. One of the reasons we must learn how to pray is that there are struggles in this world between warring principalities, and humanity can be caught in the middle. Yet Paul tells us there is a way through for followers of Christ: putting on the full armor of God. In reality, Jesus *is* the armor, and every follower of Christ is to find their strength by being in Christ. Jesus is the belt of truth and the breastplate of righteousness. Jesus becomes the shoes on our feet, leading us to the places where we are to proclaim his gospel of peace. All of this is possible by having faith in the One who will do it. By and through our faith in Jesus Christ, the flaming arrows of the evil one will be quenched. For the people of the Ephesian church, and for all of us, putting on the armor of God and standing firm becomes possible when we accept the gracious gift of salvation provided for us by the work of Christ. The result is a life empowered by the presence of the Spirit and a knowledge of Christ that grows through study of the Word and a life of prayer.

Unfortunately, we often venture out into life without putting on Jesus first. This happens when we fail to spend time in prayer. It's easy to become comfortable in our Christian walk and think, *I've got this!* Then comes the day when we are slammed by the unexpected. In that moment we realize we are unprepared and have been walking this Christian walk without the armor of Jesus Christ. We are unable to answer the tough questions, and our anxiety, fear, and frustration may get the better of us. Our responses are not Christlike, and we do not reflect Christ to the world. Recently, a friend of mine suggested praying on the full armor of God every day.

Just as we get dressed each morning to go out into the world, we should also take the time to intentionally put on Jesus. What happens as a result is attentiveness to truth, or a seemingly uncanny sensitivity to our surroundings. The breastplate of righteousness covers our heart, protecting us from the motivations and temptations that may drive us in the wrong direction. When putting on our shoes, we can begin to pray about where they may take us that day—or to whom they may lead. We become prepared to declare the gospel of peace at any destination. We pray for a firm faith, undeterred by the voices of doubt. Daily, the shield of faith is reenergized as we focus on Jesus. After we have prayed intentionally to put on Jesus, we open the written Word, soaking up knowledge of the living Word. There is something powerful and synergistic about prayer and the study of the Word. After we are prepared for the day, we discover that the Spirit gently guides and leads us as we journey through the hours. Paul knew that he needed this kind of guidance to do the work he was trying to accomplish. Why would it be different for us? We need to put on Jesus, through prayer, now more than ever.

———o———

And pray in the Spirit on all occasions with all kinds of prayers and requests. With this in mind, be alert and always keep on praying for all the Lord's people. Pray also for me, that whenever I speak, words may be given me so that I will fearlessly make known the mystery of the gospel, for which I am an ambassador in chains. Pray that I may declare it fearlessly, as I should.

—Ephesians 6:18–20

Immediately after admonishing the Ephesians to put on the full armor of God, Paul moved into prayer. Paul himself came to prayer with a deep theological understanding that grasped the significance of the gospel and shaped his emphasis on the importance of prayer. There is a gospel of peace that is at odds with the world, and there is cosmic unity that is to be experienced in the church. There are forces that are directly at odds with God's desire for believers and the church. Paul was encouraging the church toward a spiritual understanding that would create a heightened awareness of the need to pray. When the Spirit moves, the church is to pray—not only for the people who are part of the church but also for others. Prayer begins with praise to God and then moves to supplication—or intercession—on behalf of people's needs. Petition is when we pray for God's grace to be extended to us because we recognize that our own behaviors have created distance between ourselves and God.

Paul knew that his preaching needed the empowerment of the Holy Spirit. He also recognized that his faith would grow within a community of faith. This meant he depended on his fellow believers in Ephesus to become partners in his ministry through prayer. Their prayers would help him have wisdom and clarity when the time came to speak the mystery of the gospel. He wanted to be able to declare this gospel with boldness, but he knew he couldn't do it on his own. When we connect prayer to the armor of God like Paul did, something powerful begins to happen in our understanding of living a life in Christ. The more we grow spiritually, the more we realize how much we need prayer. The more we pray, the more we grow spiritually. It all goes hand in hand, and if we don't know how to pray, we will not know how to live as disciples of Jesus Christ.

I'm a person who likes background noise. However, I've found that this preference sometimes prevents me from hearing or sensing God's leading. I find direction when I find a quiet space and begin to listen and communicate with God in prayer. This is often true when it comes to my speaking or preaching. On an intellectual level, I can prepare material. However, something radically different happens when that material becomes infused with God's presence and leading. Often, in prayer, I have moments of insight that surprise me. In prayer I sense God's peace about a particular direction I am going in a project. God's leading helps me to have meaningful conversations with others. In prayer I'm prompted to contact someone or pray for a need. I need prayer because I need to be connected to God.

So how do we pray?

- We take the time to be grounded in the Word.
- We soak up every bit of learning and theological preparation that we can.
- We stand firm in the armor of God and then lean into all that God has provided for us, and journey into God's holy presence.
- We pray in the Spirit, not out of our intellect.
- We ask the Spirit to lead and guide us in new directions and toward new insights.
- We pray for our sisters and brothers who are in the midst of spiritual battles. When we are sensitive to

the Spirit, we will actually sense and know when this is happening.

- We will pray for boldness to speak the prophetic words of God to the world—yes, for ourselves, but we also pray for others to receive holy boldness.

We begin with praise and adoration of God on high. We intercede for others. We pray for our own spiritual well-being. Finally, we pray for a bold proclamation. This is the model that Paul has prepared for us, a church that shall be called a house of prayer.

Practicing Praying the Armor of God onto Ourselves

Before heading out for the day, take a few moments to pray on the full armor of God.

1. Pray that you will have faith to stand firm in the face of challenges.

2. Ask the Lord to fasten the belt of truth around your waist. We live in a world that challenges our understanding of truth. We need God's truth to lead, guide, and strengthen us every day.

3. Ask the Lord to fasten the breastplate of righteousness onto your chest. The arrows of the enemy will come to attack your heart—including your motivations and your emotions. Every day we are challenged to make good decisions based on righteousness. We pray for this protection in decision-making.

4. Pray that your feet will be prepared and ready to take action at a moment's notice so that we may be participants in God's gospel of peace.

5. Pray for strength to pick up the shield of faith that can extinguish the attacks of the evil one. We need the Lord to increase our faith on a daily basis because we recognize that the evil one will try to attack everything we believe in, encouraging us to

denounce our faith. Pray that your shield of faith will protect you.

6. Finally, pray on your helmet and sword, for you are heading out into a world of spiritual warfare. With the helmet of salvation, we hold onto the truth that we are saved by faith, and the sword at our side—the Word of God—is our defensive weapon.

2
JESUS TEACHES
US TO PRAY

———○———

And when you pray, do not be like the hypocrites, for they love to pray standing in the synagogues and on the street corners to be seen by others. Truly I tell you, they have received their reward in full. But when you pray, go into your room, close the door and pray to your Father, who is unseen. Then your Father, who sees what is done in secret, will reward you. And when you pray, do not keep on babbling like pagans, for they think they will be heard because of their many words. Do not be like them, for your Father knows what you need before you ask him. This, then, is how you should pray: "Our Father in heaven, hallowed be your name, your kingdom come, your will be done, on earth as it is in heaven. Give us today our daily bread. And forgive us our debts, as we also have forgiven our debtors. And lead us not into temptation, but deliver us from the evil one." For if you forgive other people when they sin against you, your heavenly Father will also forgive you. But if you do not forgive others their sins, your Father will not forgive your sins.

—*Matthew 6:5–15*

The disciples asked Jesus to teach them how to pray. In this setting we find a specific teaching from Jesus. He didn't instruct the disciples what to do *if* they prayed. Instead, he told them what to do *when* they prayed! With this simple word, Jesus made it clear that prayer should be an active and vital part of the life of anyone who follows him. Obviously, Jesus's perspective on prayer was different from the religious leaders of his day. For Jesus, who prayed regularly, prayer was the result of a relationship with the Father. Jesus's prayers were intimate conversations, which is why Jesus would go to meet with the Father in quiet, private places. For the other religious leaders, prayer was a way to show the world how spiritual they were. There was nothing intimate or relational about their prayers. They prayed loudly so everyone could hear. Jesus said they already had their reward because what they wanted was public honor and praise from those around them. True disciples desire a quiet, deep, intimate relationship with the Father of all creation. We are invited to spend quiet time in prayer. When alone, we are to pray following the pattern Jesus laid out for us. Prayer is not optional for a true follower of Christ who seeks a deeper spiritual life. Prayer is how we grow in our relationship with the Father, developing greater intimacy, just as Christ did.

Far too often we think of prayer as a way to talk to God about our requests when, in reality, prayer is about our own transformation. It is in the place of intimacy with God that we can hear God speak and allow God to shape us to become more reflective of Christ. Day after day, Jesus intentionally spent time with the Father. His prayer life was how he remained connected to his Father, knew the Father's will, and received power to fulfill the mission that was laid out before him.

God is asking all of us to be workers in the kingdom, but it's hard to be an ambassador if we never spend time with the King. We have become so busy these days that we expect sporadic and inconsistent five-minute prayer sessions to care for our deepest needs. Sadly, that will never be enough for us to be the followers of Christ God needs in this day and age. Somehow we need to recapture the spirit of prayer that earlier generations embraced. So, *when* we pray, we are to find a quiet place that fosters intimacy with the Lord. Then we allow Christ to mentor us, teaching us how to pray.

Our Father

Reach out to our heavenly Father with a heart of love. Worship and praise our Father for tenderly loving us as his children.

Who Art in Heaven

Worship the one who is in heaven—the Creator of all things. Our Father is the one who has accomplished all that is necessary for our salvation!

23

Hallowed Be Your Name

Holy is the name of the Lord. This loving and holy Father calls all people into his holiness.

Your Kingdom Come

We are not supposed to just sit around waiting for the day when Christ will come again, but we are to be praying for the kingdom that is already here. *Today* may his kingdom come. *Today* may we participate as ambassadors in his kingdom. *Today* may we catch a glimpse of the kingdom here on earth. *Today* may someone be touched by the kingdom. Pray for those who need to come to the kingdom, and remember to pray specifically for those who need to know Christ.

Your Will Be Done on Earth as It Is in Heaven

Jesus submitted to the will of the Father because they were in such intimate communication with each other that the Father's will was Jesus's will. We are to do the same. Pray that we would know him so intimately that we desire to fulfill his will here on earth, for his will becomes our will!

Give Us This Day Our Daily Bread

Only here do we begin to pray for personal requests, and our request is for what we *need*, what will sustain us—not what we *want*. And it is for this day—not what we need tomorrow or next week, but today!

Forgive Us Our Trespasses as We Forgive Those Who Trespass against Us

May we live lives of forgiveness. We will make mistakes, we will hurt others around us, and relationships will be damaged, but may we forgive and find forgiveness, constantly reaching out to others around us in the power of the Holy Spirit.

Lead Us Not into Temptation but Deliver Us from Evil

Praying about temptation is a healthy practice because it makes us more aware of the things that may become temptations for us. It may also prompt us to take action and stay away from things we already know are temptations. Too many times we fool ourselves into believing we are strong enough to live in the midst of that which tempts us most. That is foolish! We must admit our weakness to God and allow him to lead us in a different direction.

For Yours Is the Kingdom and the Power and the Glory Forever

The new kingdom that Jesus talked about is eternal. The kingdoms of the earth will fall away, but God's kingdom will last forever, and God will have all the power and all the glory. Worship the King today. Pour out your heart in glorious praise to him.

It's not *if* you pray—it's *when* you pray. Let's make up our minds that we are going to be a people of prayer. Added to that, let's also be a people of the Word, for the Word is teaching us to pray. When we combine prayer with Scripture, we will discover a divine synergy that will help mold and shape us into Christlike disciples.

———o———

When he saw the crowds, he had compassion on them, because they were harassed and helpless, like sheep without a shepherd. Then he said to his disciples, "The harvest is plentiful but the workers are few. Ask the Lord of the harvest, therefore, to send out workers into his harvest field."
—Matthew 9:36–38

On another occasion, Jesus looked out over the multitude of people who had been following him, and he was moved with compassion because the people had been living under a burden of religious oppression that led them to feeling "harassed and helpless." No matter what they did, they couldn't seem to get things right, and they were exhausted from trying. Jesus, the Good Shepherd, realized that no one was caring for these people or concerned about their spiritual welfare. No one was shepherding them; instead they were being used and abused by the system. In this moment Jesus told his disciples, "The harvest is plentiful, but the workers are few." Many people were spiritually hungry, but they were not being fed by the spiritual system of the day, which left them wandering. Jesus recognized that there were few who had compassion on the true needs of the people. For those disciples who would move away from the religious system and focus on the genuine needs of the crowds—on those things that moved Jesus to compassion—there would be a huge harvest. The prayer for laborers was a prayer that God would move more shepherds to compassion, recognizing the real needs of the sheep. The sheep needed Christ, not a religious system.

Jesus was moved to compassion for the real needs of the crowds, and the true shepherd works to care for the real needs of the sheep. The sheep in Jesus's day didn't need guilt heaped upon them from a religious system. I'm not sure the situation has changed much today. It's easy for church leaders like myself to get caught up in the religious system and its function, losing track of the real needs of the sheep. We are tempted to focus on what we view as perceived needs, but there is a real world around us with hurting people who have a real need to know Christ—not a religious system or structure. Jesus wondered whether there was anyone who had compassion or concern for those who needed to know Christ. Today, many lament small harvests. Could it be that there are not enough shepherds with compassion or concern for the real needs of the crowds? Could it be that we the laborers are focused in the wrong direction?

If we honestly pray for laborers for the harvest, the Lord will raise up shepherds who are moved with compassion for those who need Christ. That's where we need to begin—not with the sheep but with the shepherds. May God help us pray for the workers. May God help us raise up good shepherds. May God help us have eyes to see and ears to hear the real needs of the people. We need a whole new generation of shepherds who will have compassion and concern for those who need Christ. This is where Jesus tells us to begin to pray, for our eyes to be opened to the rich fields ready to be harvested that are all around us.

———○———

> They went to a place called Gethsemane, and Jesus said to his disciples, "Sit here while I pray." He took Peter, James and John along with him, and he began to be deeply distressed and troubled. "My soul is overwhelmed with sorrow to the point of death," he said to them. "Stay here and keep watch."
>
> Going a little farther, he fell to the ground and prayed that if possible the hour might pass from him. "Abba, Father," he said, "everything is possible for you. Take this cup from me. Yet not what I will, but what you will."
>
> Then he returned to his disciples and found them sleeping. "Simon" he said to Peter, "are you asleep? Couldn't you keep watch for one hour? Watch and pray so that you will not fall into temptation. The spirit is willing, but the flesh is weak."
>
> Once more he went away and prayed the same thing. When he came back, he again found them sleeping, because their eyes were heavy. They did not know what to say to him.
>
> —Mark 14:32–40

Interestingly, Mark's Gospel includes the encouragement to stay awake and alert because we never know when Christ will return. This scripture also tells us to be awake but this time for another reason, for now it has to do with prayer. Throughout the Gospels we find a pattern in Jesus's prayer life: he often went to a secluded area to pray for the night and invited the disciples to come with him. We are not sure as to whether the disciples actually joined him in prayer or if they were simply along for the journey. This final night in Gethsemane is an example. Jesus was, very specifically, going to the garden to spend time in prayer. He asked the disciples to come with him and to keep watch. The problem was, they did not pray; they simply fell asleep. And this pattern was repeated two more times.

The disciples were constantly learning about prayer from Jesus. They began their prayer lives in rudimentary ways. They watched Jesus pray and finally one day had the courage to ask Jesus to teach them to pray. That's when they received the instructions for the Lord's Prayer. It appears, however, that, until Jesus left them, they really did not develop much of a prayer life. After he ascended into heaven, they became hungry for the fellowship they had experienced with Christ. The entire group of disciples was willing to go to the upper room and spend ten days in prayer, waiting for the coming of the promised Advocate— the Comforter, the Holy Spirit. As their relationship with Jesus grew through the Spirit, so did their prayer lives. As for us, we may start small, or we may begin by falling asleep when trying to pray, but we must press on. We must make time to fellowship with the Lord in prayer. Maybe we begin with the Lord's Prayer, but with diligence and faithfulness, we will expand beyond that framework as we begin to touch the heart of God. As a result of their prayer lives, the disciples were transformed by the Holy Spirit. We too can be transformed, but we must be willing to spend time in prayer. For Jesus, it was a priority. He knew he could do nothing without talking to and being in fellowship with the Father.

To reexamine the Gethsemane scenario, Jesus took the disciples with him to this garden that probably had a cave-like area where they could be protected from the wind and other potential elements. He told the disciples to sit while he prayed, but then he took Peter, James, and John with him a little farther, to the place where he wanted to pray. Jesus was agitated because he knew what was coming. When he returned, he found the disciples sleeping. He was not only concerned for himself but also cared about what was going to happen to his disciples. He urged them to stay awake, keep watch, and be in prayer. Jesus knew they would need the strength that comes from God to endure the difficulties ahead. If they pressed on in the power and strength from on high, God would help them through the upcoming trials in the days ahead.

The problem with the disciples was that they were stumbling in their weakness. Their spirits certainly wanted to participate with Christ, but their flesh was weak. Our hearts and minds may want to be engaged in God's work too, but we live in human bodies that can bring us down. The flesh is weak, and we can stumble in that weakness.

It seems there are times when we conveniently connect the spirit and the flesh and times when we choose not to! However, how we live our lives in the flesh is a reflection of our life in the Spirit. We may think we want to live for Christ, and our spirit may be willing, but then we fail to make the connection with how we live day in and day out.

Christ knew the flesh was weak and that it would cause problems for the disciples—and also for you and me. There are many stumbling blocks we will encounter, and our physical weakness is something we need to bring before the Lord. At the same time, our physical weaknesses may also need to be infused with some self-discipline. If we are too tired, we will be tempted. If we are not eating in healthy ways, we will be tempted. If we are not putting the right things into our minds, we will be tempted. We all have weaknesses that the enemy would like to use to become our stumbling block. Jesus knew this and was warning the disciples. Prayer and self-discipline would go a long way toward helping them in their spiritual journey and in overcoming temptations. We are encouraged to remain alert and pray so we don't stumble over our weaknesses.

———◇———

Returning the third time, he said to them, "Are you still sleeping and resting? Enough! The hour has come. Look, the Son of Man is delivered into the hands of sinners. Rise! Let us go! Here comes my betrayer!"

—Mark 14:41–42

We learn much about Jesus and his posture of prayer during this Gethsemane scene. It was common for people of the Jewish faith to pray aloud, so the words recorded here would have been what Peter remembered and shared with Mark. Normally a Jewish person would stand before God, arms raised toward heaven, and pray aloud. Instead, this passage shows Jesus in great distress, throwing himself on the ground and pleading with the Father that the hour might pass from him. The use of the Aramaic word *Abba* is placed here so that we understand the intimacy between Jesus and his Father. Children commonly referred to their fathers as *Abba*, and disciples used the word as one of respect in reference to an esteemed teacher.

While Jesus's prayer was simple, it was also intense. He was in deep distress over the coming events and preferred not to have to face the cross. This was his human nature—not wanting to have to go through what was coming. Yet, in obedience, he would follow through and accept what lay ahead. In this way Jesus conquered the enemy. This entire passage is another lesson on prayer. We see Jesus's bearing, and we are allowed to hear his intimate address, which included a confession of God's omnipotence. Jesus pleaded to be spared from suffering and then declared his obedient submission to the will of the Father. What we see in his posture is his helplessness apart from the Father's enablement for the mission. Although he prayed for deliverance, he also accepted the suffering. Having laid himself out before God, he would be able to stand before humanity.

We find ourselves crying out to God in the difficult circumstances of life. Unfamiliar circumstances lead us to the model we find in Christ, who lived in a posture of submission to the Father. We cry out to the Father in our pain, confessing that life is beyond our control, yet "not my will, but yours be done." We learn to live with a submissive posture before the Father, and then we can stand and serve humans. We are invited to participate with Christ in intense prayer during times of acute distress.

Learning to Pray the Lord's Prayer

Find a quiet place without distractions and begin to spend time following Jesus's example of prayer:

1. **Our Father**. Begin by soaking in the relationship that we have with a loving heavenly Father. He is our *abba*, our dad, and he wants the best for us and is always ready to listen. Worship and praise our Father for tenderly loving us as his children.

2. **Who art in heaven**. Take a few moments to worship the one who is in heaven, the Creator of all things. Think about the beauty of the things that surround you, and thank God for his creative hand in all things.

3. **Hallowed be your name**. Pray that God's name might be holy in this world. God's nature reflects holiness, and if God's name is made holy, then we see the sanctity of all that God has created. Ask God to open your eyes to his holiness and to his holy desires for you and your life.

4. **Your kingdom come**. Pray that God's kingdom would come now. Pray for ways in which you may serve as an ambassador in God's kingdom. Specifically, pray for those who need to know Christ and enter the kingdom. You may want to make a list of these individuals and pray for them on a regular ba-

sis. Include family members and loved ones as well as acquaintances.

5. **Your will be done on earth as it is in heaven**. Pray that you might be able to enter into the intimate relationship found in the triune God and there come to know the heart of the Father. Pray that you might get to know the will of the Father so you can join in praying for God's will to be done on earth.

6. **Give us this day our daily bread**. Now we may begin to pray for personal requests. Remember, we are to pray for needs, not wants. Also pray for what you need *today*, not for tomorrow or next week. Keep focused on the present and on what you need for God to sustain you in this moment.

7. **Forgive us our trespasses as we forgive those who trespass against us**. Pray that you might live a life of forgiveness. Ask the Lord to reveal your own mistakes, and be willing to say you are sorry. Pray to live a life of forgiveness toward others.

8. **Lead us not into temptation but deliver us from evil**. Pray that God would make you aware of the temptations around you. Pray for wisdom to deal with temptations. Admit your weaknesses, and ask God to help lead you away from the areas of life that may be a temptation.

9. **For yours is the kingdom and the power and the glory forever**. Give God praise for the new, eternal kingdom. Finish your time of prayer in worship of God, who is eternal, pouring out your heart in glorious praise to him.

3

PRAYER AND PARTICIPATION IN THE MISSION

---◇---

Yet the news about him spread all the more, so that crowds of people came to hear him and to be healed of their sicknesses. But Jesus often withdrew to lonely places and prayed.
—Luke 5:15–16

Quietly tucked into Luke's narrative, we find what may very well be the secret to Jesus's ministry: he was busy day in and day out doing the Father's business. Miraculous transformations were occurring in the lives of numerous people: the blind could see, those with leprosy were healed, the paralyzed could walk, and the crowds were following him everywhere. Yet even Jesus knew that his strength had to come from his fellowship with the Father. He had to withdraw and be alone so he could pray.

I lead a pretty busy life—yet my life is nothing like that of Jesus Christ. I can't imagine what it must have been like for him, continually ministering to so many needy people. He was constantly giving of himself to help others, to help them see and envision the kingdom of God. It was exhausting work. Yet even Jesus could not do it alone. He made it a priority to get away and spend time in prayer.

Jesus's entire life on this earth was one that revealed sanctified humanity. Jesus came so that we too could be holy. His life became a demonstration for us of the work that God wants to accomplish in and through us. For that to happen, we are to follow the example of Christ—to imitate him. If Jesus needed to withdraw on a regular basis "to lonely places" in order to pray, then we need to as well. We are all juggling the busyness of life, but the busier we are, the more time we need to spend with him! Somehow this time of withdrawal needs to become a regular part of who we are, just as it was with Christ. We need to create deserted places where we can simply be alone with him; in doing so, we will receive the wisdom and strength that can only come from him. After this, we are able to return to the chaos of our lives. Withdrawal became a pattern for Jesus. Luke tells us that he did it "often," implying that Jesus found prayer so important he intentionally made himself inaccessible. To be able to spend the time that Jesus needed in prayer, he had to stop preaching, teaching, and healing and get completely away from people to spend time alone with the Father.

Sometimes we set up a dichotomy and begin to argue over which is more important in our spiritual lives: getting to know Christ or participating in Christ's mission in the world. The reality is that we need both, and in getting to know Christ, we can then join with him in participating in his mission. But the only way we will really get to know Christ is by spending time with him, which means we have to make knowing Christ a priority in our lives, which means prayer has to become a priority. One of the most revealing things about Jesus's earthly activity was that he intentionally withdrew to pray. There were always people who needed to be healed. There were always people who wanted to hear him preach. He could have worked 24/7 and still not reached everyone, yet he intentionally established boundaries for his personal life.

If we are going to get to know Christ and be empowered by uniting with him, then we have to be intentional about our prayer life. We have to withdraw from everything else and spend time alone with Jesus. If Jesus had to do this, how much more so do we? Jesus had to spend time with the Father, and in doing so, the Father's passions became his passions, and the Father's strength became his strength. The Father's desires were his desires. The result was Jesus's very effective ministry.

Slow down. Take time to withdraw to pray. The work will still be there, but—just like Jesus—we will be recharged and able to tackle our work better when we are more focused and empowered by God.

After this, Jesus went out and saw a tax collector by the name of Levi sitting at his tax booth. "Follow me," Jesus said to him, and Levi got up, left everything and followed him.

Then Levi held a great banquet for Jesus at his house, and a large crowd of tax collectors and others were eating with them. But the Pharisees and the teachers of the law who belonged to their sect complained to his disciples, "Why do you eat and drink with tax collectors and sinners?"

Jesus answered them, "It is not the healthy who need a doctor, but the sick. I have not come to call the righteous, but sinners to repentance."

They said to him, "John's disciples often fast and pray, and so do the disciples of the Pharisees, but yours go on eating and drinking."

Jesus answered, "Can you make the friends of the bridegroom fast while he is with them? But the time will come when the bridegroom will be taken from them; in those days they will fast."

—Luke 5:27–35

Luke is the only Gospel author who identifies Levi as a tax collector. The significance of this story is the calling of Levi, his past, and the way Jesus responded to him. This man answered the call from Jesus and threw a great banquet for him, where all the sinners of the community could come to fellowship. For the religious leaders of the day, this event was appalling. For Jesus, it was an incredible opportunity to be in the midst of a group of people who were in need of the Great Physician. The religious leaders didn't understand the importance of Jesus's table fellowship. Instead, they condemned him for his activity, instructing him and his followers to pull back, separate themselves from these sinners, and spend time in prayer and fasting. In that moment Jesus brought up the story of the wedding feast and the bridegroom. No one fasts during a party! This wasn't the time for prayer and fasting; it was the time for table fellowship, where people like Levi could be awakened out of their unbelief.

Dr. Hans Rohling, originally from Sweden, served in community health in Mozambique. His area of specialty was infant mortality, and he wanted to help treat as many babies as possible. He began studying the statistics of his community and discovered that, while some babies died in the hospital where he worked, hundreds more were dying in the community. Many of his colleagues challenged his assumption that his energy would be better spent improving community health, thereby dropping the overall infant mortality rate. His friends wanted him to stay in the hospital and use all the latest technology to save a few lives. He thought he ought to go out into the villages and homes and try to change the living conditions so fewer babies overall would come to the hospital. Eventually he was able to change the culture of the community, and the lives of hundreds of children were saved every year—but his actions were not without controversy.

When we spend all of our time in the church (like Dr. Rohling's hospital), making it as nice as it can be, we may only be reaching a few sick individuals a year. Yes, we may be able to bring everything to the forefront to help them, and we see may see in them great transformation, but what about the hundreds in our communities who are dying? Just like the Great Physician did, we need to go find the sick. That means looking for opportunities of table fellowship with those whom religious officials may find offensive. There are times when we are called to fast and pray, but fasting and prayer are supposed to empower us toward table fellowship. Then we must pray that our table fellowship experiences become moments where the unbelief of those like Levi will be awakened.

———○———

"But to you who are listening I say: Love your enemies, do good to those who hate you, bless those who curse you, pray for those who mistreat you. If someone slaps you on one cheek, turn to them the other also. If someone takes your coat, do not withhold your shirt from them. Give to everyone who asks you, and if anyone takes what belongs to you, do not demand it back. Do to others as you would have them do to you.

"If you love those who love you, what credit is that to you? Even sinners love those who love them. And if you do good to those who are good to you, what credit is that to you? Even sinners do that. And if you lend to those from whom you expect repayment, what credit is that to you? Even sin-

ners lend to sinners, expecting to be repaid in full. But love your enemies, do good to them, and lend to them without expecting to get anything back. Then your reward will be great, and you will be children of the Most High, because he is kind to the ungrateful and wicked. Be merciful, just as your Father is merciful.

—Luke 6:27–32

In the middle of the Sermon on the Plain (Luke's truncated version of the Sermon on the Mount that is found in Matthew), Jesus laid out what kind of responses were to come from those participating in the new kingdom. Life in this new kingdom was and is to be countercultural. These teachings were not like anything the disciples had ever heard before, and Jesus's sermon left them wondering. The Israelites, to whom he was speaking, had been looking for political solutions to their problems. Not only had they looked for political answers, but they were also willing to use force when necessary. Jesus cautioned them that those who are part of his kingdom should have a completely different response. Instead of fighting off enemies, Jesus said they were to love them. Instead of building up weapons of war, they were to look for ways to do good toward those whom they hated or who hated them. Not only were they to do good for their enemies, but they were even to go so far as to bless and pray for them.

The kingdom of God functions on many different levels. We live within the kingdom on a personal level, or sphere. There will always be those who can find fault in us and won't like us. How will we respond to them? There have been times in my life when I have had a defensive, almost visceral response to people like this—but then there is the moment when I take a deep breath and recognize the call for a kingdom response. We are to be like Christ and live as ambassadors of God's kingdom. It is not our prerogative to vindicate ourselves, and Jesus said to expect nothing in return from those who may be our enemies. Nothing! He has instructed us to simply do good and realize that our reward is not here on this earth but in heaven.

As the corporate body of Christ that lives and operates within the kingdom, we must also be concerned with communal responses to our enemies. What would Jesus expect the kingdom response to be for the church? Do the rules of the kingdom suddenly change, or are we also to love our enemies, bless them, and pray for them? It seems pretty clear that this is Jesus's command—not only to his individual followers but also to his bride, the church.

The final verse of this passage sums up the entire command with the statement, "Be merciful, just as your Father is merciful." The structure of this sentence reminds us of the mirror command from the Old Testament to be holy as God is holy! What connection is there between holiness and mercy? Could it be that, for us to be the holy people of God, we are to learn how to show mercy? It seems this would be true if the goal of holiness is Christlikeness. The kingdom of God that Jesus ushered in is a kingdom in which we are invited to respond as Jesus would respond. Yes, it turns everything upside down and should make us stop and think, realizing that life within the kingdom is radically different from life in the world. Unfortunately, we have at times accepted the justifications of the world around us and tried to adopt them into the kingdom. There were times when there was nothing rational about Jesus's preaching. That irrational kingdom is the one into which we are now invited to live and participate, and this participation comes about by prayer. Jesus knew the disciples' hearts were to be transformed by prayer, and in this way they would become God's holy, merciful people.

———○———

Then Jesus told his disciples a parable to show them that they should always pray and not give up. He said: "In a certain town there was a judge who neither feared God nor cared what people thought. And there was a widow in that town who kept coming to him with the plea, 'Grant me justice against my adversary.'

"For some time he refused. But finally he said to himself, 'Even though I don't fear God or care what people think, yet because this widow keeps bothering me, I will see that she gets justice, so that she won't eventually come and attack me!'"

And the Lord said, "Listen to what the unjust judge says. And will not God bring about justice for his chosen ones, who cry out to him day and night? Will he keep putting them off? I tell you, he will see that they get justice, and quickly. However, when the Son of Man comes, will he find faith on the earth?"

—Luke 18:1–8

To participate in Jesus's mission means there will be persistence in prayer. In this parable the widow never gave up on the judge because she believed that eventually justice would be served. As followers of Jesus Christ, we are to have faith that we serve a God who hears our prayers and believes in justice. Prayer is one of those great mysteries that may be difficult to comprehend, yet we learn from this parable that we are to persist in prayer. Somehow, as the woman continued to cry out, her prayer was answered. If God knows what we need before we even ask, then why does God want or need his people to cry out to him in prayer? There is much more at stake in this parable than just a woman's need being met. She needed to be saved from her adversary, but the question was really about the greater mission of justice. Through her persistence, the one who had the power to change her circumstances became engaged in bringing about justice. What we see from the judge is that the persistence of the woman led to his participation in her mission. For disciples, our persistence results in participation in the Father's mission.

This idea of persistence may seem dated, but there is great power in prayer. More than fifty years ago, the denomination I serve was struggling financially. During the month of January, the leadership of the denomination came together to talk about the mission of the church, and in this season following World War II, they weren't sure how the mission would continue. Instead of going home one night, several of the leaders decided to spend time with the Lord in prayer until they got an answer. Four or five of them stayed and began to labor before the Lord in persistent prayer. The group included the general treasurer, the missions director, and others. Some stretched out on the floor before the Lord, crying and pouring out their hearts. They persisted in prayer until, in the early morning hours, they believed they had heard from God about a way forward. In those quiet hours the Lord laid out a plan for giving across the denomination that would fund the mission for years to come, up to and including the present day. I often wonder what would have happened if those leaders had not been willing to sacrifice themselves in persistent prayer. It's easy to cry out to God in a moment of need, but there must also be an ongoing relationship by way of a vital prayer life. Those who stayed up all night in prayer were experienced prayer warriors. When things got tough, they knew that they needed to linger in God's presence and seek God's wisdom. They had practiced persistence.

There is nothing in our human behavior that changes God's nature. God, in his grace, is constantly reaching out to us, wanting to draw us near. However, he is asking that we join the stream of his grace—or the movement of his Holy Spirit—through a life of prayer. This is one of the mysteries of heaven that we do not comprehend, but when God's people unite together in prayer, things are loosed in heaven that have been bound up. Does God need humanity to participate for this to happen? No—because God is all-powerful. However, God desires human participation and has established an order for us to unite with him through prayer.

If we examine historically all the great revivals or awakenings that have occurred, it has been when God's people have prayed. Significant time has been spent in prayer—not just a few moments here and there. Rather, there has been a persistence, a getting hold of God and not letting go until the power of the Holy Spirit has been poured out and there has been a significant movement or shifting here on earth. All disciples are to adopt a lifestyle of persistent prayer. Simply crying out to God when life gets difficult will not produce the kind of sustaining grace that we need in our lives. Jesus wants all of his disciples to adopt a lifestyle of persistent prayer, not just intermittent cries to God when life gets rough.

We are living in a crucial time for our world and certainly for Christianity. The cultural and social shifts we see around us are simply astounding, and we may wonder what the future holds. Unless Christians unite together within the power of the Holy Spirit through prayer, we will not have a chance when we come under attack from the forces of evil in the world. We must cry out for God to have mercy on us, for we have been unfaithful!

When Jesus shared the parable of the unjust judge, his disciples may have been tired and felt defeated. There would already have been those attacking them and their ministry. It would have been easy to lose heart and become frustrated, so this parable was a piece of pastoral guidance. David A. Neale tells us, "The challenges of life as a church in a hostile world is [the disciples'] daily reality. This appears to be the situational lens through which we should understand the Christian community Luke addresses."[1] He goes on: "Human prayer and actions matter to God. The result of human activity is not predetermined. An ardent and holy heart can move God to action. In today's world of widespread suffering, questions naturally arise as to the efficacy of prayer. Why should we pray? Does it really make a difference? The Gospel of Luke encourages us to see ourselves as significant actors, agents of free will who can help shape the course of events through holy intervention in prayer."[2] Did you catch that? *Human prayer and actions matter to God!* This parable is about how you and I will continue to press on through life. There will always be times of disappointment and difficulty. We will feel like we are losing heart, but in those moments we are to persevere in prayer and action. Prayer is the lifeblood of the disciple, both past and present.

Don't give up! Hold onto that deeply personal relationship with Jesus Christ. Persevere in spending time with the

1. David A. Neale, *Luke 9–24: A Commentary in the Wesleyan Tradition,* New Beacon Bible Commentary (Kansas City, MO: Beacon Hill Press of Kansas City, 2013), 170.
2. Neale, *Luke 9–24,* 171.

Lord, sharing with him from your heart, and he will hear and answer. The answers will encourage your heart and help you see the justice of God, not the justice of humanity, and in the meantime, we may discover that we are the ones who are transformed. The answer to our prayers may be within ourselves, and that is where God will find faith on earth. There is nothing we can do for the sake of the kingdom that is not bathed in prayer, and when it feels like the prayers aren't being answered, we should continue to storm the gates of heaven. Gather friends and family around you to join you in prayer. Do not give up, and do not lose heart. Pray always, for this is as necessary for a disciple of Jesus as the air we breathe.

Praying for our Participation in the Mission

1. Find a quiet place where you can spend undistracted time in prayer. Embrace time in prayer as a priority.

2. Pray for God's leading into action and participation in the mission. Ask God to open your eyes to those who need him. Pray for boldness to leave our secure places and go to those who need Christ.

3. Practice persistence in prayer. You may want to set a timer and pray for five minutes. Gradually build that time up, five minutes at a time, until you are able to spend an hour in prayer with the Lord. Set aside a regular time to pray every day. You may need to add it to your calendar so the time is blocked off and becomes a priority.

4. When faced with a difficult circumstance, don't give up, but persist in prayer. It may take days, weeks, months, or even years.

4
POSTURE IN PRAYER

————o————

To some who were confident of their own righteousness and looked down on everyone else, Jesus told this parable: "Two men went up to the temple to pray, one a Pharisee and the other a tax collector. The Pharisee stood by himself and prayed: 'God, I thank you that I am not like other people—robbers, evildoers, adulterers—or even like this tax collector. I fast twice a week and give a tenth of all I get.'

"But the tax collector stood at a distance. He would not even look up to heaven, but beat his breast and said, 'God, have mercy on me, a sinner.'

"I tell you that this man, rather than the other, went home justified before God. For all those who exalt themselves will be humbled, and those who humble themselves will be exalted."

—Luke 18:9–14

On the heels of the parable of the persistent widow, Jesus continued his teaching, making an example of two men and their posture in prayer. Our demeanor in prayer speaks volumes about our faith. The woman in the previous parable was impassioned in her need. We too must be impassioned about the needs around us, going to God with those needs daily and pouring out our hearts. At the same time, we should not be discouraged. We may not get the response we think we want at that very moment, but God is listening to our heart's cry.

Jesus realized there were those in the crowd who were proud of their spiritual lives. There was the Pharisee who had been following all the rules, including paying his tithe. Doing right things is important, but good works are not to be used to justify one's place before God. The Pharisee trusted in himself and his own ability rather than in God. He was feeling self-sufficient about his faith because of the pride he had in his religious practices and good works. He even told God how good he was, and this was his problem. As Jesus continued to teach, he reminded the disciples that not only were they supposed to learn how to pray, but their attitude and character in prayer were also of great importance. In this way Jesus was teaching them about the character and behaviors that are appropriate in the kingdom of God. Basil of Caesarea, a fourth-century church leader in Cappadocia, wrote about this passage and the lessons to be learned:

Be on your guard, therefore, and bear in mind this example of grievous loss sustained through arrogance. The one guilty of insolent behavior suffered the loss of his justice and forfeited his reward by his bold self-reliance. He was rendered inferior to a humble man and a sinner because in his self-exaltation he did not await the judgment of God but pronounced it of himself. Never place yourself above anyone, not even great sinners. Humility often saves a sinner who has committed many grievous transgressions.[1]

The great sinner, presented by way of contrast, was a tax collector. There weren't many people in Jewish society who were hated more than the tax collectors. Tax collectors paid the Roman government for a permit to collect taxes. A certain amount was due to the government annually for this permit, but anything they could take above and beyond this fee was theirs to keep. They were blessed with wealth for their notorious corruption. The Jewish people felt that tax collectors compromised with the local government in order to use and abuse their own people. In a sense, there was a special category of hate and resentment reserved for the vile behavior of the tax collector. Yet in Jesus's parable he was the one who humbled himself before God. He understood that he was entirely undeserving of grace. Grate-

---

1. Saint Basil the Great of Caesarea, "Homily on Humility," https://www.johnsanidopoulos.com/2020/02/homily-on-humility-st-basil-great.htmlhttps://www.johnsanidopoulos.com/2020/02/homily-on-humility-st-basil-great.html.

ful for all that God had done for him, he trusted in God alone for his salvation.

Our posture before God reveals our place of trust. Years ago, I took a course in personal evangelism. I remember a discussion on saving faith. Our professor used a chair for his illustration. He asked if we believed that the chair could hold us up. The chair looked sound enough from where I was sitting. Then he asked us to prove whether the chair could hold us up. The only way for me to do that was to get up out of the chair I was sitting in and go sit in the other chair. This was his illustration for saving faith; we can't just believe in Jesus, but we must put all of our lives into his hands, trusting him entirely for salvation. The posture was visible for all to see. Either I was sitting in my old chair, or I had moved to the new one. My posture revealed my place of trust.

It's easy to take much for granted when we have been in the church for a long time. Eventually, living for the Lord, having devotions, paying our tithes and offerings, and going to church can become routine. If there isn't a freshness in our hearts, we can become like the Pharisee who trusted in himself. When we begin to trust in ourselves and think we are sufficiently righteous, we will be tempted to tell God what to do. God's children are invited into a holy relationship in which we are continually gripped by the grace of our Lord and where we live in humility, for we are overwhelmed by the presence of Christ, who sits at the right hand of the Father. In the throne room of God's presence, we discover that depending on ourselves is folly. Worship of our Creator alone is what sustains us.

I'm afraid churches may be filled with those who believe they are righteous before God because of what they have done personally. Good people are tempted to stand before God and demand a particular response because of how they've lived. It's that temptation to tell God that my child must be healed because I've been good; or to tell God that, because I've been faithful, my business must succeed; or that my marriage should be perfect because I've worked hard at loving God and my spouse. We can slip into the place of the Pharisee quite easily, and Jesus was fully aware of that possibility.

We are all sinners saved by grace. Even if we've been walking with the Lord for many seasons, we are to come before God in humble gratitude. The cry of our hearts is that God would have mercy on us. We are absolutely unworthy of his goodness. God's love and mercy are gifts to us. That is why he tells us to come to him like little children. We approach in innocence and faith, believing that we may humbly sit on his lap, and ask, "Can you forgive me?" As we cry out, the Lord hears our cries and he answers our prayers. We discover that prayer is a practice of life within the kingdom of God. In this place, our character is shaped and hewn into the image of Jesus. That's why our posture in prayer is vital. Going to church and participating in a religion can make us religious, but it may not make us like Christ. The call to discipleship is formational, both inside and out. We have to be careful that we don't simply conform to outward expectations of what it means to be spiritual. The person the world sees is formed in the intimacy of prayer, and if we are not spending time in prayer, we are allowing ourselves to be shaped and formed by the things of this world. The character of our prayer life will, in fact, shape our character. To be a genuine follower of Jesus Christ requires an attitude of submission in God's presence, where we are shaped into the image of Jesus Christ.

———◇———

*Then he prayed, "L*ORD*, God of my master Abraham, make me successful today, and show kindness to my master Abraham. See, I am standing beside this spring, and the daughters of the townspeople are coming out to draw water. May it be that when I say to a young woman, 'Please let down your jar that I may have a drink,' and she says, 'Drink, and I'll water your camels too'—let her be the one you have chosen for your servant Isaac. By this I will know that you have shown kindness to my master."*

—*Genesis 24:12–14*

In Genesis we find the story of the servant who was sent by Abraham to find a wife for Abraham's son Isaac. In this passage the servant referenced his "master" on numerous occasions. His posture in prayer was one of great respect for both his earthly and heavenly master. There is no question whom he served. The entire mission was done on behalf of his master, and his focus was on doing this work well, with the help of God. The servant was incredibly wise as he lifted up this prayer to the God of his master. He had come to know and understand the heart of his master and realized a young woman would need to fit into his master's household. His prayer reflected this knowledge because he knew his master was generous and hospitable. Against the common response of human nature, he prayed for a young woman who would share her water and also go the extra mile by watering the camels as well. He believed that God's love for Abraham would be revealed by providing a young woman who would have a heart like his master's, ready to reflect the family values by the way she lived her life. The focused way in which this man served reflected his relationship with his master. The servant knew the heart of his master so well that he knew exactly how to pray.

This is the type of intimate relationship with the Lord that we are to have, dwelling in God's presence day in and day out, so much so that we begin to know and understand the desires of God's heart. This is a posture of continual prayer. When we know the desires of God's heart, then we know how to pray. The servant's prayer reflected great intentionality. He knew what the master needed, so he prayed for it directly. Do we know what God needs? Would we know how to pray for that need directly? These are challenging questions for us because the ability to pray is directly related to our intimacy with the Lord.

The servant was able to serve well because he knew and understood the master's needs. Success in the eyes of the world is not necessarily faithful service to God. If we fail to understand the ways of God, we may find ourselves praying for the wrong things—or not praying at all. We are tempted to run out to do the Master's work without first getting instructions from the Master. What if the servant had brought back the wrong girl? All of history would have been altered. Probably the most important decision in this story is not the girl but the selection of a faithful servant to do the work of the master. God is still looking for faithful servants who will serve the Master well. In great humility, often without the leading role, the faithful servant seeks the well-being of the Master, evidenced by the posture taken in prayer, and ultimately glorifying God.

———○———

Is anyone among you in trouble? Let them pray. Is anyone happy? Let them sing songs of praise. Is anyone among you sick? Let them call the elders of the church to pray over them and anoint them with oil in the name of the Lord. And the prayer offered in faith will make the sick person well; the Lord will raise them up. If they have sinned, they will be forgiven. Therefore confess your sins to each other and pray for each other so that you may be healed. The prayer of a righteous person is powerful and effective.

—James 5:13–16

James provides us with a pattern for our posture in prayer. This is also a pattern for our spiritual growth and development. First of all, there will be suffering among those who are followers of Jesus Christ. If we are to be like him, then we will also suffer as he suffered. How did Jesus respond to suffering? He prayed! He spent time talking with the Father, and we are to do the same. In the midst of the difficulties that life sends our way, we are to spend time with the Father in prayer. In this posture of prayer, we are to bring to him our needs and requests. Jesus was not alone in the garden of Gethsemane. He brought his burdened heart and laid it before the Father, from whom he received strength and power to move forward and fulfill the purpose for which he had been sent.

What about those who are cheerful? There are times in life when things are good and we are experiencing God's joy, peace, and love. Yes, times can be good, and in that juncture of life, we need to simply embrace it as a gift from the Lord. In the midst of the good season, take time to praise God and allow him to shine through in the good. Don't think that you don't need God just because things are going well. Rather, rejoice and embrace what God is doing in and through you. Be cheerful and let the music roll!

What happens when someone becomes ill? They are to call together the leaders of the church, who are to pray over them and anoint them with oil in the name of the Lord. This is reflected in the community of faith that comes together, uniting in prayer over the needs of one who is ill. Something synergistic happens when God's people get together to pray. And not just synergistic but also exponential; therefore, the community is called together to be a united front in praying for the healing of the sick. The anointing oil is symbolic but may also be a form of treatment. Ointments and balms were often used as medical treatments for healing. It could be that we see the community coming together to pray while at the same time applying necessary medical treatment. God can use the two together to bring about healing.

The promise was for miracles to be witnessed by those who prayed. Within the community of faith there would be those who would be healed of their sicknesses, both physically and spiritually. The elders laid hands on those who were sick, and forgiveness of sin was occurring for those who were willing to confess their sins. Accountability in the community of faith led to a time of prayer, and those leading the prayers were righteous. This is why they saw the results they did from the powerful and effective prayers of a community of faith. They prayed, they praised, they anointed, and they confessed. This is certainly a pattern we should emulate today. The posture of prayer moves beyond the individual and into the corporate. Intentionality in corporate prayer is needed, and this ought to be reflected in our worship services, demonstrating our corporate priority of prayer.

Some may wonder about miracles and whether we experience them today as they have been experienced in the past. Could it be that we are not experiencing miracles because we are not practicing prayer, praise, anointing, and confession on a regular basis in our communities of faith?

Could it be that we are not genuine *communities* but merely *individuals* who gather together on Sunday morning to worship but are not interconnected throughout the week or in the rest of life? These instructions are to be lived out *within* the community of believers. In this we find support and accountability, which lead to a powerful and effective prayer life.

Practicing our Posture

1. When you begin to pray, ask the Lord to check your attitude. Allow the Lord to examine your heart and illuminate motivations that are not from the Lord.

2. Ask the Lord to give you a spirit of humility, both in prayer and when dealing with others.

3. When you sense the Lord convicting you of something, bring it to him immediately in prayer. Be willing to repent and ask God to forgive you.

4. Practice corporate prayer within a community.
   a. If you have a nuclear family, establish prayer times together, preferably every day. Pray together at mealtimes and before bed.

   b. If you are part of a small group, make sure to set aside times when you pray together.

   c. Join a group of people who are committed to praying together. Schedule a time to meet together regularly for prayer.

   d. If you are a pastor, practice prayer among your people in worship and in other group settings. Keep anointing oil ready.

   e. Never leave a hospital visit without praying for the person you are visiting.

5
PRACTICING WHAT WE'VE BEEN TAUGHT

———○———

In Joppa there was a disciple named Tabitha (in Greek her name is Dorcas); she was always doing good and helping the poor. About that time she became sick and died, and her body was washed and placed in an upstairs room. Lydda was near Joppa; so when the disciples heard that Peter was in Lydda, they sent two men to him and urged him, "Please come at once!"

Peter went with them, and when he arrived he was taken upstairs to the room. All the widows stood around him, crying and showing him the robes and other clothing that Dorcas had made while she was still with them.

Peter sent them all out of the room; then he got down on his knees and prayed. Turning toward the dead woman, he said, "Tabitha, get up." She opened her eyes, and seeing

Peter she sat up. He took her by the hand and helped her to her feet. Then he called for the believers, especially the widows, and presented her to them alive. This became known all over Joppa, and many people believed in the Lord.

—*Acts 9:36–42*

Jesus had returned to the Father, and it was up to the disciples to practice what they had learned from him. In this season the reputation of Christ's apostles was growing, and people began to call upon them when they had need. Tabitha was a good woman who devoted herself to helping others. She was gifted with her hands and used her talents and abilities to help those in need. Sadly, she seems to have died quite suddenly, and her small community was distraught. Her friends and loved ones heard that Peter was nearby, so they called for him. Immediately he came and discovered what an amazing woman she had been. The people wanted him to know everything she had done for them. The widowed women, without financial support, were grateful for the beautiful things she had created for them. One can only imagine the joy of a simple yet beautiful piece of clothing when one had nothing else, and this was what Tabitha provided.

Peter knew they were suffering, but he sent them outside while he remained alone with the body. He quieted himself, then knelt down and began to pray. The rest of the scene unfolded as he spoke to her, telling her to get up. Amazingly, her eyes opened, and she sat up. This miracle was retold on numerous occasions, and many believed in Jesus because of it.

It's interesting to focus on Peter in this whole scenario. He prayed, seeking to know where God was leading, and something transformative happened in that time and space. God's plan is for us to be transformed into the image of Christ—for us to be reflections of Christ in this world. This is holiness: we are to be like our holy God, participating with God as we live our lives in the world. It's easy to skip over the significance of Peter taking time to pray in the story, but in that moment we see him slip into participation—and then transformation—with Christ.

What we see happening in the middle of the story is a change in focus. Tabitha was known for her good works. Her life was a testimony because of the good things she had done. Peter's goal was not to do good works—his goal was to become like Christ. After praying, he turned to her body and used her Aramaic name, Tabitha. If he spoke the entire sentence in Aramaic, his words would have been only one letter different from the words that Jesus spoke when he raised the little girl from the dead: *"Talitha cum."* Now Peter spoke and said, *"Tabitha cum."* In that moment we look at Peter and don't know if we're seeing Peter or if we are seeing Christ. This is the call of the Christian life—a life of holiness that leads us out into mission.

As the disciples began to practice the life of Christ, they spent intentional time in prayer. This time in prayer led to participation in the life of Christ. We are to be partakers of the divine nature, transformed by his holiness, which will always lead us to mission, and it all happens when we start with prayer.

———○———

So Peter was kept in prison, but the church was earnestly praying to God for him.

The night before Herod was to bring him to trial, Peter was sleeping between two soldiers, bound with two chains, and sentries stood guard at the entrance. Suddenly an angel of the Lord appeared and a light shone in the cell. He struck Peter on the side and woke him up. "Quick, get up!" he said, and the chains fell off Peter's wrists.

When this had dawned on him, he went to the house of Mary the mother of John, also called Mark, where many people had gathered and were praying. Peter knocked at the outer entrance, and a servant named Rhoda came to answer the door. When she recognized Peter's voice, she was so overjoyed she ran back without opening it and exclaimed, "Peter is at the door!"

"You're out of your mind," they told her. When she kept insisting that it was so, they said, "It must be his angel."

But Peter kept on knocking, and when they opened the door and saw him, they were astonished.

—Acts 12:5–7, 12–16

Peter continued to follow the example of Jesus and was engaged in the Lord's ministry. As a result of this work, he was arrested and put in prison. Already a small church had formed, and the people of that congregation knew exactly what to do: they went to prayer. One evening, as the group was holding a prayer meeting, an angel came to Peter in prison and set him free. He then made his way to the home where the people were praying. The likelihood is high that the folks at the prayer meeting were praying for Peter and his freedom. The irony is that, while they were praying, he arrived at the home. The servant Rhoda was so excited at hearing his voice and realizing their prayers had been answered that she forgot to let him in. Instead, she ran to tell the others, but those praying failed to recognize that the answer to their prayers was standing right outside the door, and they told Rhoda she was out of her mind. Even while they were doing what they had been taught, they still couldn't believe that God had answered their prayer.

What are our expectations when we pray? It seems we are often surprised when God answers prayer. That seemed to be the case with those praying for Peter. Even though they had gathered to pray specifically for this need, they were shocked when the prayer was answered. This story speaks to our *attitude* when we are engaged in prayer. Do we pray believing that God can make a difference? God can and does make a difference in our lives. Prayers may not always be answered in the way we expect or hope, but God does care and respond. Sometimes we simply have to open our eyes to see what God has already accomplished and will continue to do in and through us and those around us. Enter into prayer expecting that God will answer! Then be open to the creative ways in which God may want to respond, and don't be shocked when he does!

―――○―――

About midnight Paul and Silas were praying and singing hymns to God, and the other prisoners were listening to them. Suddenly there was such a violent earthquake that the foundations of the prison were shaken. At once all the prison doors flew open, and everyone's chains came loose. The jailer woke up, and when he saw the prison doors open, he drew his sword and was about to kill himself because he thought the prisoners had escaped. But Paul shouted, "Don't harm yourself! We are all here!"

The jailer called for lights, rushed in and fell trembling before Paul and Silas. He then brought them out and asked, "Sirs, what must I do to be saved?"

They replied, "Believe in the Lord Jesus, and you will be saved―you and your household." Then they spoke the word of the Lord to him and to all the others in his house. At that hour of the night the jailer took them and washed their wounds; then immediately he and all his household were baptized. The jailer brought them into his house and set a meal before them; he was filled with joy because he had come to believe in God―he and his whole household.

―Acts 16:25―34

Paul and Silas were locked up in prison because of their faithful obedience to God. Instead of being angry or taking it out on the jailer, they prayed and sang hymns to God. They kept their eyes on the goal of knowing Christ, and they didn't let the frustrations of the day distract them from what was most important. The result was that not only were their spirits lifted, but they also ministered to others around them. God worked through an earthquake, and many were saved both physically and spiritually.

The book of Acts, even with the difficulties that the disciples faced, is always full of hope. Therefore, when Paul and Silas found themselves in prison, they used it as an opportunity to pray and worship the Lord in the presence of the other prisoners. They realized that their imprisonment was not about them but was about the way God could use them to reach others. So they praised and glorified God, even in chains.

Suddenly there was an earthquake, and on the heels of Peter's miraculous deliverance from prison by the angel, we might assume the earthquake that threw open the doors of the prison and loosened all the prisoners' chains was meant to deliver the freedom of Paul and Silas. But Paul and Silas—and God—had something else in mind. Instead of running free immediately, they stayed put, along with their fellow prisoners. This was not a typical response. God was up to something. As we find out, it seems God wanted to use the earthquake not primarily for Paul and Silas's deliverance but for the deliverance of the jailer.

Paul and Silas waited patiently. They did not run from the jail; instead, they calmed the nerves of the jailer, who feared for his own life at the prospect that he might have fallen asleep and let a whole prison full of captives escape.

As a result of Paul and Silas's caution and patience, deliverance came to the jailer and his entire household. In that moment God was glorified, and lives were transformed. Paul and Silas understood that this situation was not just about them. They knew they would have to suffer in order to reach those whom God wanted them to reach. In patient obedience they withstood all that came their way and allowed their troubles to deliver others.

Often in the life of the church, we focus on the spiritual development of individuals, perhaps precluding our ability to see the ways our lives are meant to intersect with the lives of others. We are not islands unto ourselves; our actions have implications for others, including our prayer lives. When we live in a constant posture of prayer, we may discover that God wants to use our circumstances to become a blessing for others. This perspective takes us beyond our individualistic way of thinking and raises within us the passion of our Lord to seek and save the lost. Jesus was engaged in an active, not a passive, process of salvation. When we become united with Christ, his passions become our passions, and we are driven by the desire to do all that we can to be like him. We can imagine that Jesus would have been in that jail—and, in fact, he was! Paul and Silas were willing, just as Christ was, to give themselves up as living sacrifices for the sake of the gospel.

In many countries, Christianity finds itself under threat from government authorities. At times, Christians find themselves concerned about their own personal welfare in more restrictive environments. Interestingly, even in light of government restrictions, Paul and Silas refused to capitulate because they weren't concerned with their own welfare. They didn't wait to try and invite the prisoners and the jailer to church to tell them about Jesus. They participated with Jesus in the jail cell and used their difficult but ordinary situation for the extraordinary. They were not worried about their own security but about the mission of Jesus Christ.

Paul and Silas's attitude had a great deal to do with the outcome of the situation. One can only imagine that they were tempted to be frustrated. How could God be in the midst of their being locked up in jail—and illegally! Can't you imagine the indignation and desire to let those around them know they were being held by corrupt officials? Yet they didn't reveal their legal status until the end of the story. They believed God could use their circumstance for his glory, so they chose to walk through the difficulties with a good attitude. Sitting in prison, they sang songs to the Lord. You know what happens when we sing to the Lord? Not only is God glorified, but our own spirits are also lifted because our focus becomes God and not ourselves. They were able to look to God and praise him, and others began to listen. Their unusual response provided a way out. God was praised and glorified, the earth shook, and they were set free along with the jailer. They could never have imagined this outcome, but they prayed and kept their eyes on the Lord.

There will be times when we won't be able to see where things are heading, or even where things *could* go. As far as Paul and Silas knew, their lives could end in that jail. But their goal was to reflect all they had learned about Jesus, which included praying and praising God in all circumstances.

Practicing What We've Been Taught

1. Find a quiet place for prayer so you won't be distracted.

2. When you find yourself in a difficult situation, take a deep breath and begin with prayer.

3. Pray, believing that God can and does answer prayer. Keep a record of your prayer requests, revisit them, and take note of when and how the prayers are answered. Spend time praising God for answered prayer.

4. Ask the Lord to use you to bring others to Christ.

5. Ask the Lord to help your attitude when you are faced with a challenging situation. Ask the Lord to help you see what God wants to accomplish in any given situation. Then rejoice in the fact that you have been given the opportunity to be part of the mission.

6

MENTORING YOUNG LEADERS
Praying with Paul and Timothy

———o———

I urge, then, first of all, that petitions, prayers, intercession and thanksgiving be made for all people—for kings and all those in authority, that we may live peaceful and quiet lives in all godliness and holiness. This is good, and pleases God our Savior, who wants all people to be saved and to come to a knowledge of the truth.

—*1 Timothy 2:1–4*

"I don't know how to pray!" How often do we hear this today? In the past it seems that the art of prayer was passed from one generation to the next, yet suddenly we live in a day and age when many people claim they simply don't know how to pray. In this letter to Timothy, we catch a glimpse of the expectations of a follower of Christ. All were encouraged to spend time in prayer. Mentoring the next generation is always important. We find that the apostle Paul was constantly teaching and mentoring his young leaders, including Timothy. The call to prayer was an important aspect of the life of the Christian community. They were to bring needs and requests, as well as their thanksgivings, before the Father in prayer. Prayer is meant to be a primary focus in the life of a believer. Paul is encouraging the young pastor Timothy, emphasizing that prayer must be a priority in his life and in the life of his congregation.

After this, specific instructions are given in regard to the content of prayer. There are to be supplications—earnestly asking or begging for things. There are times when supplication is necessary because the burdens we carry are so heavy. There are also to be prayers that include the worship of God. Then there are to be intercessions, where we pray for others, and finally thanksgiving, or praises lifted up to God. For whom are we to pray? For kings and queens and presidents and chancellors and all of those who find themselves in high, authoritative positions. The prayer is not that these people will change who they are but that we will be able to lead "peaceful and quiet lives."

No one should be excluded from the prayers of the church community. Even those with whom the church community does not have common interest are to be prayed for, including those in leadership over us. To pray for the leaders is to pray for the whole community because of the decisions they make on behalf of those within their sphere of influence. Therefore, it is a Christian's duty to pray for those whose actions will impact every citizen. Ultimately, prayer is to be at the heart of church life.

In my travels, I once found myself in three countries in one week. In all three of them I read the news while I was there and saw that each place had its own problems and political concerns. On that journey I stayed in a hotel where the four wives of one country's president were also staying so they could introduce a son to a royal princess. They and their entourage made quite a scene when sauntering into the dining room. Throughout this journey of life, we will all find ourselves in different places politically and with varying assessments regarding the leaders we encounter or are subject to. Some will be considered good, others bad, and our opinions of some will be indifferent. Some of us may think a leader isn't worth praying for, yet Paul's urging to pray for leaders lists no exceptions.

Different commentaries on this passage have responded in very contextualized ways. Tertullian, in the second and third centuries, was living during a time of persecution, yet he affirmed praying for leaders. The emperor and his assistants were enemies of the church, hurting the followers of Jesus Christ, yet Tertullian implored his people to pray for their persecutors. John Chrysostom, in the fourth and fifth centuries, wrote when the church was under the protectorate of the Roman Empire. Before he was born, the Roman

Empire declared that Christians should be free to worship without fear of persecution, and during his lifetime, Christianity became the official religion of the Roman Empire. Chrysostom urged his parishioners to pray for the emperor and for the decisions of the empire that would affect the lives of its citizens. The people were charged with praying that decisions would be just and would improve the welfare of all citizens. Tertullian and Chrysostom lived and wrote in different contexts, yet both imitated Paul in advising continued and ongoing prayer for those in leadership.

Whether we agree or disagree with our leaders, we are called to be people of prayer. Nothing says we have to agree with them, but we *are* commanded to pray for them. Leadership can be lonely; far too often, the only voices a leader hears are those who affirm the leader's actions because others are afraid to speak the truth. We need to pray that truth will be both spoken and heard. We must be willing to pray the very best for our leaders today because the decisions of leadership have the power to effect change for the whole community, even the world. We pray for the least of these when we pray for the most powerful. This focus on prayer helps set everything right and plays a role in the salvation of those who do not know Christ. Paul's implication seems to be that Timothy cannot be an effective leader if he does not spend time in prayer.

Prayer seems like such an ordinary act, so ordinary that sometimes we make the mistake of assuming that all Christians regularly engage in prayer. The sad truth is that we are doing little to train up the next generation in regard to prayer. In the early days of the Holiness Movement, prayer was a central theme. Here's a story about the experience of a camp meeting in 1898:

> The 6th of October, 1898, will be a red-letter day in the memory of many souls. As the people were engaged in prayer, there came upon them such a spirit of prayer that many began to pray all over the house, and there came over the assembly such tides of glory and power that several lost their strength, and little was done during the rest of that service but simply wait and praise, while such a sacred wave and heavenly glory filled the place, as it has not often been the privilege of those present to witness and enjoy.[1]

Prayer was a major feature of the gatherings of the early Holiness Movement. They took to heart the guidance found in the Word of God and prioritized prayer. Often there was more praying in a camp meeting than preaching. Today that reality is reversed, and I wonder whether the church is hurting for it.

The pattern laid before Timothy can be useful for our own prayer lives. There are times in life when we are going to need to make supplication—when our hearts are broken or so burdened that we cannot bear it any longer, so

---

1. P. F. Bresee, ed., "The Home Camp Meeting," *The Nazarene* (Los Angeles: The Church of the Nazarene, 1898). This publication later came to be known as *The Nazarene Messenger* and ran until 1911.

we pour out our cares before the Lord. This need will be different for every one of us, and its urgency may fluctuate through the seasons of our lives, but God is always waiting and ready to listen.

Prayer should *always* include praise and worship of God. Notice that requests are only part of prayer, while most of prayer is about dwelling in the presence of God. God loves us and delights in our spending time in holy fellowship with the Trinity. We simply need to slow down long enough, be still, and listen to the voice of God in humble worship.

Intercession for the needy and lost is also vital. Intercession is one of the great mysteries of God that we cannot explain, but somehow our participation in praying for those in need seems to be efficacious. Some of the early church fathers talked about the synergism—or the release of energy—that occurs when humanity participates with God. In prayer we are invited to participate with God's activity in this world. God's passions become our passions, and our hearts are broken for those who need to come to Christ. I'm not sure there can be any evangelism without prayer.

When I pray with groups, it seems people struggle the most often with thanksgiving. We may be uncomfortable with thanksgiving if we haven't practiced it and are only accustomed to bringing our requests before God. Our hearts are to be full of thanks for the things God is doing in the world, in and through us. Could it be that we have become so caught up in the negativity and criticism of our day that it's hard for us to break from that mold and actually give thanks?

We must find a way to carve out time for prayer in our daily lives. It may be helpful to make a list of those for whom we need to pray. Maybe it's something we do on a rotating basis, praying for different people, or groups of people, on different days of the week, but we need some type of plan. Praying for others includes praying for those we may not even like. We are encouraged to pray for everyone, including our leaders and those we may view as our enemies or those who view themselves as our enemies. It doesn't matter whether they are followers of Christ—we must pray for them. Only through this time in God's presence, through prayer for those with whom we have affinity *and* with whom we do not, will we find deep and amazing peace. This kind of peace gives us a life of tranquility and dignity. Now that sounds appealing, doesn't it? We must practice the *art* of prayer, filling our time spent with God with petitions and thanksgivings.

———o———

Therefore I want the men everywhere to pray, lifting up holy hands without anger or disputing. I also want the women to dress modestly, with decency and propriety, adorning themselves, not with elaborate hairstyles or gold or pearls or expensive clothes, but with good deeds, appropriate for women who profess to worship God.

A woman should learn in quietness and full submission. I do not permit a woman to teach or to assume authority over a man; she must be quiet. For Adam was formed first, then Eve. And Adam was not the one deceived; it was the woman who was deceived and became a sinner. But women will be saved through childbearing—if they continue in faith, love and holiness with propriety.

—1 Timothy 2:8–15

The people attending Timothy's church seemed to have some problems and were not behaving in a good way. Christlikeness was probably not a word people could have used to describe what they saw at the church. Therefore, Paul gave instructions to address those concerns.

The men were arguing with one another. Instead of focusing on their disagreements, Paul exhorted them to learn to pray together. When they gathered together, they were supposed to lead by praying, not by arguing.

The women were refusing to give up worldly practices. The believers in this church were being converted in a city full of secular influence. In Ephesus we find the temple to Artemis, or Diana. This temple was one of the seven wonders of the ancient world, and people came to worship, sight-see, and purchase souvenirs. Ephesus was the Las Vegas of the Mediterranean. One can imagine the influence this culture might have on the women of the city who wanted to appear sophisticated for those who visited this cosmopolitan crossroads of the world. Braided hair, gold, pearls, and expensive clothing may have represented ways that women prepared themselves to worship Diana. Now that they had confessed Christ, they didn't need to look like the women who worshiped idols made with human hands. This admonition was about kingdom life and reality.

The people were being influenced by popular theology. In a city and region where female goddess worship had become popular, the church seemed to be adapting to the local religion. Some of the women of the church had bought into a heretical idea that Eve had been created first, then Adam. This idea would certainly make it popular to come to a church in a city where they revered the goddess Diana. These uneducated individuals in the church purported to know the truth, and their heresy was becoming dangerous. Some rules had to be set down to deal with the crisis. Those who were not educated in religion and theology were not to be the ones teaching it! In this case, that happened to be the women. Jewish men would have studied the Hebrew Scriptures growing up, so Paul is giving the men a positive admonition: don't keep this knowledge to yourselves, but take the time to teach your wives at home. The women were to be given the opportunity to get to know the Word so they would no longer be enticed by false ideas. This was a problem of failed discipleship in the church. Those with knowledge should have been teaching those who did not have it.

Those who may have felt chided needed to be encouraged. The women in Timothy's church could have had their feelings hurt by these comments and instructions. There doesn't appear to be any intent to repress the women but to help them grow spiritually. Therefore, this passage ends with a word of hope that is often misunderstood, but it comes to us from the incarnation of Christ. When Jesus is born in human flesh, he provides for the transformation of all that has been corrupted. From the moment of the fall, all of creation has been groaning under the pain of corruption. Quite specifically, women bore a heavy burden for Eve's participation in the fall. The relationship between men and women was changed, as was her burden of pain in childbearing. When Jesus entered the world and touched human flesh, he revealed the hope of transformation. The first place Jesus touched humanity was in the womb of a woman. This is the good news for those who need to be encouraged. At the place of our greatest suffering, Jesus comes to bring hope and transformation. The women struggling to grow in their faith were blessed with the good news that Jesus touched a woman first and, in that act, began to reverse the order of sin.

When the situation in the life of the church becomes difficult, it's important to take time to address the real issues. Spiritual issues need to be confronted. Prayer must be a priority of the church and community. Getting to know the heart of God will keep the church from falling into disagreements. It's easy to argue over issues that become a distraction from the real work of following Christ. Prayer humbles all who meet at the foot of the cross.

To be a follower of Jesus Christ, you cannot have all the things of the world. It simply doesn't work that way. There is self-denial involved in following Christ. The extravagances of a worldly life grow dim in the light of knowing and following Christ. If that's not happening, then the focus is on the wrong things. Lot's wife continued to look longingly on the life she was leaving behind, and she lost it all as a result. Life in Christ has much more to offer than we often recognize. We talk a lot about the self-sacrifice aspect of life in Christ, which is not wrong, but there is also much to gain. It's important to focus on the positives too.

There is a desperate need for discipleship across the age spectrum within the church community. Jesus told his followers to go and make disciples, and we must be engaged in the intentional practice of helping others grow in their faith. Those who are not like us should be invited into the discipleship experience. We should have our eyes open so we can invest in the development of others, including those who may seem unlikely candidates. At the same time, we must tread lightly when dealing with relationships in the community of faith. We are to build one another up, even when nudging in the right direction. My father used to say, "Always err on the side of compassion." Never lose your loving spirit, and remind people of their unique place in receiving grace. It's a reminder to us as well, that we are recipients of undeserved grace.

Yes, there will be tough moments in life, but those who have gone before become our mentors. They leave us with a pattern for dealing with issues that have happened in the past and will happen again. We participate with those who have gone before, and with our holy God, in this spiritual journey. It is both our individual and our collective journey as we draw closer to Christ. Along the way, we are challenged to commit to a life of prayer and, in this way, reflect Christ in every circumstance, no matter how difficult.

———○———

Alexander the metalworker did me a great deal of harm. The Lord will repay him for what he has done. You too should be on your guard against him, because he strongly opposed our message.

—2 Timothy 4:14–15

Knowing that Timothy would face challenging days and difficult people, Paul offered some practical advice as well. No one is immune from those who want to cause harm. Alexander seems to have intentionally undermined the Christian ministry. The sad part is that at one point and time he apparently was part of the church but then took it upon himself to attack the doctrine and create a great deal of trouble. Considering his occupation, he was probably not well educated, and so we can imagine the great gusto with which he may have attacked the church, thinking he knew what he was talking about but in fact being terribly destructive. Sadly, many people were hurt and probably walked away from their faith in God as a result. The concern here in terms of harm was not the personal struggle or damage to an individual reputation but the fact that innocent people were being led astray.

The message from Paul is clear. There is not to be any personal retaliation. We must allow God to judge according to the person's own actions or deeds. At the same time, we are not to be ignorant of the damage these types of individuals may be able to do. We must be wise and no longer give them space to continue to do harm in the church. All the while, we continue to pray for them. Most of us will have an experience where someone may not like us or tries to make our lives difficult. It's not our job to get back at them. There is a graciousness that must come from growing in our walk with the Lord and spending time in prayer. When we witness those who harm others, we need to think and pray about a wise response. We cannot allow individuals to come into the center of our fellowship and destroy the faith, especially for new believers. It would appear that, for Paul, trying to talk to this individual and resolve the misunderstanding didn't help matters, and that will often be the case for us as well. There will always be some who are not willing to hear or learn and will be dogmatic about what they believe. They may also damage your personal reputation, but that is not the greatest danger. Let them hurt our reputation; only let us beware, and protect those whom they may lead astray. Love and pray for those who choose to undermine you, and let God take care of paying them back.

Learning from our Mentors

1. Seek out someone who knows how to pray. Ask them if you might join with them in prayer on a regular basis—maybe once a month to start.

2. Make a list of the people for whom you need to pray. You may want to make a schedule, praying for different people on certain days of the week or month.
   a. Family members

   b. Friends

   c. Specific/stated needs

   d. Leaders

   e. Those with whom you may not agree/enemies

3. Practice gratitude. Make a list of all the things you can be thankful for. Spend time praying these thanks to the Lord.

4. Pray for situations that may cause division or dissension within or among God's people. Ask God for wisdom to respond to the challenges.

5. Pray again for those who may be a challenge for you to love or who may be actively causing problems for you.

7
PRAYER AS FOUNDATIONAL TO SPIRITUAL GROWTH
Paul and the Ephesians

---○---

I keep asking that the God of our Lord Jesus Christ, the glorious Father, may give you the Spirit of wisdom and revelation, so that you may know him better. I pray that the eyes of your heart may be enlightened in order that you may know the hope to which he has called you, the riches of his glorious inheritance in his holy people, and his incomparably great power for us who believe.

—*Ephesians 1:17–19a*

Paul's letter to the church in Ephesus is full of practical helps for believers who are living in a secular world.

Ephesus was a city at the crossroads of civilization, blessed with the temple of Diana. Here, Paul planted a church that Timothy would later pastor. Trusting in Jesus as Lord was a new concept to these followers, not to mention a threat to the leadership of the Roman Empire. There was much they had to learn, including how to pray.

Often, in the midst of a letter, Paul would break out into prayer. His prayers offer us particular insights into the longings of his heart and what he saw as the needs of these new disciples. Reading Paul's prayer for the Ephesian Christians is enlightening. As their spiritual father and mentor, he knew what they needed in their lives, and his greatest concern was for their spiritual growth and development. In the first chapter Paul named three things that are necessary for continued and ongoing spiritual growth and development of new believers.

A Spirit of Wisdom

Paul's desire was for these disciples to come to know God through wisdom. God's wisdom, visible in Christ Jesus, is provided through the Holy Spirit. By living in the power of the Holy Spirit, the spirit of wisdom is received, and this allows us to come to know God. Those who love God are drawn closer in fellowship, thereby experiencing his nature.

A Spirit of Understanding

Through the presence of the Spirit, minds are opened to the wisdom of God, which leads to greater understanding. Faith in Jesus Christ may seem foolish to the world, but it is transformational in the life of the believer. This transformation reveals to us the the glorious hope we have of adoption into the family of saints. The spirit of understanding opens minds to recognize the calling from God to reflect Christ in this world. The inheritance is for all to embrace as adopted children of God.

An Experience of Power

The power of God was already at work in the life of the Ephesians, and the true God was able to do far more than the goddess of Ephesus. The power that Paul embraced was resurrection power, transformational power, adoption power—the kind of power to make the Ephesians into saints of God!

Paul knew that spiritual growth and development were vital in the lives of the Ephesians, so it was his prayer for them. Paul's prayer raises the question: What did you pray for today? Our prayer lives can become consumed by our lists, which are important but not the sole purpose of prayer. We aren't supposed to briefly mention someone's name in prayer and move on—we are to follow Paul's example and pray for them by need. He recognized the spiritual need among the people, so he prayed that they would know Christ in a deeper and more intimate way.

Paul prayed in the Trinity, acknowledging the role of the Father, Son, and Holy Spirit and the need for full participation in this holy relationship. We come to know God by participation in the triune God. That is the goal—to know God. As a result, our eyes are opened and our hearts enlightened. Then we see the true hope that we receive through Christ. The glorious inheritance is the kingdom for those who have been adopted as children of the King. There is more power in that kingdom than we recognize, and Paul knew that his children in faith needed to learn how to tap into what God made available.

We live powerless Christian lives when we fail to spend time in fellowship with the triune God. What does that look like? Sometimes it's just sitting in silence and quieting our spirit to listen. What would happen if we turned off the TV, the internet, the music—and just listened? Some of my best moments with God are on airplanes, flying far above the earth with no distractions. Suddenly it seems I hear the voice of God. I don't know how many sermons have come to me in those moments of quiet—whole messages that it just seems God is downloading into me. That doesn't happen when I'm wrapped up in noise. Be willing to slow down and be quiet. During a quiet morning in the Democratic Republic of the Congo, I experienced God in the lapping of the water, the morning mist across Lake Kivu, and the occasional gecko crawling up the wall. Every now and then a fish broke the surface and appeared on the water. In this stillness and beauty, I was awestruck by the Creator.

Pray that you may experience the power of the Holy Spirit at work in your life and in the lives of others. The supernatural power of God is still at work in this world. Sometimes we fail to see or experience the Spirit because we become too consumed with our own lives. Next, be willing to take upon yourself the ministry of intercession for others. This Paul did exceedingly well because he was willing to carry the burden for those whom he had brought to Christ. He actively discipled and mentored others, and this included praying for them.

———○———

For this reason I kneel before the Father, from whom every family in heaven and on earth derives its name. I pray that out of his glorious riches he may strengthen you with power through his Spirit in your inner being, so that Christ may dwell in your hearts through faith. And I pray that you, being rooted and established in love, may have power, together with all the Lord's holy people, to grasp how wide and long and high and deep is the love of Christ, and to know this love that surpasses knowledge—that you may be filled to the measure of all the fullness of God.

—Ephesians 3:14–19

Paul's deepest desire for the church was that it would be spiritual and passionate about Christ. His emotions came to the surface as he poured out his heart in prayer. He did not pray for the charismatic gift of the church, but he prayed that the church would be the dwelling place of Jesus Christ. The connection between the Spirit and Christ is clear, for you cannot have one without the other. Christ must dwell in their hearts, and only when this happens will God's people be strengthened by the power of the Spirit.

There is no Spirit without Christ, and there is no Christ without the Spirit.

Paul's prayer was that the church be made up of individuals who had spiritual passion because Christ dwelt in their lives. The more one grows in Christ, the more that life rests upon Jesus, the Cornerstone, and the greater the power through the Spirit. Paul's desire for the church was to experience the riches of his glory and be strengthened. These things are only possible through faith, when Christ dwells within. The result is that there is no room left for anything that may be hostile to God.

There are many things we can focus on in the life of the church, but if we don't begin with a deeper spiritual life, we have a problem. Just like the apostle Paul, our prayer ought to be for a depth of spirituality that profoundly changes who we are. Everything about us ought to be defined by our relationship to Jesus Christ. If we truly grasp what Paul was saying, then Christ is to permanently make his dwelling place within us. The body of Christ will then be made up of those who unite together and who have, by faith, made space for Christ to live in them.

What's interesting to me is Paul's passion. His heart was almost breaking as he cried out to God on behalf of this church, that the people would have a deeper walk with Jesus Christ. He knew that a surface relationship would not be enough. Far too often our churches are focused on the surface—on getting people in the door, not on the deeper walk. If we were to be honest with ourselves, we may discover we haven't made disciple-making the priority that it was for Paul. Paul was never satisfied with his own spiritual status, nor with that of those whom he mentored in the faith. He knew there was always more, so he pressed on toward the goal. He lived a life of faith that continually wanted to know more of Christ. Living in the status quo would never have been acceptable to Paul, and neither should it be for us.

The church is to be a place where those who seek a deeper walk with Christ are bound together in holy love. Living in Christ results in a life empowered by the presence of the Holy Spirit, bringing about radical transformation, not only in the life of the sinner but also in the one who is entirely sanctified yet wants to know Christ and embrace resurrection power. The riches of God's glory are available to be experienced in the church not through charismatic worship but by a deep indwelling of Christ. Christ becomes the one who brings passion to work and ministry. Paul challenges us to examine our own spiritual passion and whether we have truly embraced Christ through faith. It's a giant leap—not just once but continually as we live in the power of the Spirit.

———○———

Pray also for me, that whenever I speak, words may be given me so that I will fearlessly make known the mystery of the gospel, for which I am an ambassador in chains. Pray that I may declare it fearlessly, as I should.

—Ephesians 6:19–20

We have been blessed by the prayers of the apostle Paul and the way in which he prayed for those whom he discipled. His prayers have reached through the centuries all the way down to us today, but now we find this twist. He asked that those at the church in Ephesus would also pray for him. He recognized that he needed prayer support from them just as much as they needed it from him. Paul gave them specifics: he wanted them to pray that he would have a message to speak about the mystery of the gospel. Jerome, a church leader in the fourth century, said this should be understood as if Paul had said, "Let the treasuries be opened. Let the promises hidden from ages be revealed. Let the Spirit enter to bring forth those things that have been concealed."[1] That is a powerful prayer, and not just a good message to preach but also one that reveals the hidden promises of God.

At the same time, Paul requested prayer for boldness, but this boldness needed to be tied to his own spiritual life. Origen said, "Boldness of speech is a possibility only and always for those who have a heart that does not condemn them . . . and therefore the one who boldly makes known the mysteries is rare, because those who have boldness before God are rare."[2] Therefore, this simple prayer request from

---

1. Jerome, "Epistle to the Ephesians" in Ronald E. Heine, *The Commentaries of Origen and Jerome on St Paul's Epistle to the Ephesians* (Oxford: Oxford University Press, 2002).

2. Origen, "Epistle to the Ephesians" in Heine, *The Commentaries of Origen and Jerome on St Paul's Epistle to the Ephesians.*

Paul was profound, and we can begin to understand the reason for it. While he prayed earnestly for the Christ followers of Ephesus, he himself was in desperate need of their prayers for him. If Paul, the great missionary and apostle, needed this type of prayer support—how much more do we? God still needs followers today who will preach with boldness the mystery of the gospel. I'm afraid that, at times, messages that are preached today are filled with cute anecdotes and illustrations yet fail to be bold when it comes to unlocking the promises hidden from the ages. The message is not supposed to draw attention to the one who is proclaiming but instead should point toward the deeper mysteries of God. That's what makes the statement of Origen so profound. This prayer of Paul was not just for his words but that he himself would be the man with a pure heart that he needed to be. Paul's request is a challenge to us as well. If we are to proclaim boldly the mysteries of God, we too must have pure hearts.

All of this brings us to the humble recognition that we need the fellowship of the saints. We need to be in relationship with other Jesus followers who will be praying for us. We pray for them and they for us. This reciprocity in prayer should happen in every community of believers. Paul was passionate about praying for the Ephesians, and he needed them to be passionate about praying for him.

Practicing Prayer with Paul

1. Pray for your own spiritual maturity, that you may have the Spirit of wisdom, of understanding, and an experience of power.

2. Pray for the ongoing discipleship of those around you.

3. Pray for the eyes of your heart to be enlightened. Practice silence. Begin by spending one or two minutes in silence and to listen. Eventually, try to expand this time to five minutes, then ten.

4. Read Scripture reflectively. Don't try to hurry through your study of Scripture. Read a smaller section and ask God to teach you something through what you have read.

5. Listen carefully when people preach and teach. Pray that God will help you learn something new. Take careful notes!

6. When you encounter a servant leader, watch carefully and see what you can learn from their life.

7. Try to follow the example of those whom you recognize as being close to the Lord.

8
THE NECESSITY
OF PRAYER

———○———

Devote yourselves to prayer, being watchful and thankful. And pray for us, too, that God may open a door for our message, so that we may proclaim the mystery of Christ, for which I am in chains. Pray that I may proclaim it clearly, as I should.

—Colossians 4:2–4

In these final words of instruction to the church in Colossae we discover what is really important in the eyes of Paul for Christ followers. They are to be devoted to a life of prayer—but not a prayer life that dulls the senses. Instead, they are to be committed to a prayer life that makes them alert. Prayer is to be filled with thanksgiving and intercession, and while praying for others, we are to pray for doors to be opened to spreading the word so the message may be clearly understood.

While we've been studying what Scripture teaches us about prayer, we still have to wonder whether we really understand what prayer is all about. Many of us have experienced a so-called prayer meeting in which there was very little prayer. We may have also experienced a time of prayer requests that some have called an "organ recital"—where every need stated is related to a physical ailment. Paul wanted us to understand that prayer is about so much more—it is about who we are, for we are to be a people of prayer. At the same time, our churches are to be houses of prayer.

Prayer is about spending intimate time in the presence of Jesus, and through this intimacy in prayer we are transformed. That's why Paul thought it was so important to encourage the people in Colossae to be a people of prayer. To experience the transformative power of the Holy Spirit working in our lives, we too must be a people of prayer. Spirit-filled transformation will help us be alert to what is happening around us. This transformation includes being attentive to temptations that may appear at a moment's notice, or the Spirit may help us notice doors of opportunity that are open before us to spread the mystery of Christ. Being engaged as a faithful follower of Christ requires us to be alert! At the same time, we are to have a spirit—or attitude—of thanksgiving, which means we should come before the Lord with our praises and words of thanks. How often do we do that? I'm afraid not very often. We jump right into the bunion prayer requests. What would happen if we turned our prayers around and spent most of our time in thanksgiving instead of in petition? That would be transformational! It's *meant* to be transformational because God is to be praised and worshiped and thanked in our prayers.

Finally, many people tell me they have never led anyone to the Lord, nor would they know how. The secret is right here in what Paul had to say. Paul said to make it a matter of prayer. I'm guessing one reason we don't make it a matter of prayer is that we are afraid God might answer the prayer, and then we'd have to speak up! But if we make sharing Christ a matter of prayer, we might be surprised by the doors that open and the words God gives us to speak. Usually it takes very little on our part, for the Holy Spirit does the work in the heart of the individual.

As Christ followers, we are to be devoted to prayer. We must make prayer a priority in our lives, for without it we will die spiritually. If the Word of God is our spiritual food, then prayer is the breath in our lungs. We might be able to go without food for a short period of time, but if we do not pray, we will be suffocated by the things of this world. The exhortation to prayer wasn't meant to be a harsh command from Paul but life-giving advice, for devotion to prayer is the solution for life.

———○———

Now may our God and Father himself and our Lord Jesus clear the way for us to come to you. May the Lord make your love increase and overflow for each other and for everyone else, just as ours does for you. May he strengthen your hearts so that you will be blameless and holy in the presence of our God and Father when our Lord Jesus comes with all his holy ones.

—1 Thessalonians 3:11–13

Over and over again Paul's own personal life is an example to us. Much of his time was devoted to prayer, and his articulated prayers leave us with beautiful templates of what motivated him in private conversation with God. Notice that he prayed to God the Father *and* the Lord Jesus. Paul revealed to us his experience of the triune God in prayer. Our prayers ought always to be directed to God *through* Jesus Christ, who intercedes for us. Through this intercession, the Holy Spirit leads and provides direction.

Paul's opening in prayer reveals his pathway to God, and then we find Paul's actual request. His prayer for the Thessalonians was that their lives would increase and abound in love for one another. Remember, Jesus said the world would recognize his followers by their love for one another. Paul knew this love from God had to be present in the lives of the believers. Therefore, he prayed for this love to be lavished on God's followers, so much so that it would pour out over the entire congregation. Not only was this love to abound within the congregation, but it was also to spill out and touch the world around them. This love was for all to experience. Paul set himself up as the example, for he had been praying for this love to be revealed in his own life. His heart was overflowing—abounding—in love for these, his spiritual children.

Once we recognize the importance of praying to God and acknowledge that we are to pray for abounding love, the final verse helps us place it all in context. Jesus lived and died to make us holy. The goal for all of humanity is to be transformed into the nature of Christ, which is holy love. That's why Paul's final plea in prayer was that their hearts may be strengthened in holiness. This over-abounding love reveals the nature of Christ in you and in me. It means we are being strengthened in holiness, and if transformation in holiness is why Jesus came, then we become blameless before God as we grow in him. This entire prayer is one in which the followers were being drawn up into God's eternal plan for all humanity. We are to be transformed into the likeness of his image—to become more and more like Jesus Christ. Jesus's life abounded in love. The manifestation that Christ is at work in us is that we will abound in his love toward those within the community of faith as well as toward the world around us. This is true holiness.

I had the privilege of visiting a church in the city of Toronto. This church had at least six different congregations from varying cultures meeting within the same building or facility. The place was active from morning until night, filled with people from across the spectrum of society. The kitchen and gym were used to feed fifty teens from the community. Another room was used to teach parenting skills to twenty women. Another section provided childcare for the moms who were learning to better care for their children. The afterschool program was training the teens in life skills. Soon I saw the worship team arrive for practice: a group of people who mostly came from the Caribbean. Downstairs I saw a mix of the congregations that had gathered for a prayer meeting, for a mighty outpouring of love among this diverse group. The place was bursting with people coming to praise and worship and serve God.

On our way home that evening, we were discussing what it must be like to try to organize some of this holy chaos throughout the building. The pastor mentioned that, when he first arrived, the building was deathly silent. He said you could hear the crickets! Now he is filled with joy at the noise and laughter that fills the halls. Have there been challenges? Of course! The wear and tear on the building is visible, and not everyone always cleans everything up. Yet the pastor's wife said, "But it's in those moments that you realize that you can show the love and grace of God to others as you wash their dishes." That's love abounding to one another. That's love overflowing to all. That's the incarnational power of holiness—and isn't that really the goal? We join with Paul in praying for God's love to overflow not only for one another but also for everyone else.

———○———

Rejoice always, pray continually, give thanks in all circum-stances; for this is God's will for you in Christ Jesus.
                                                    —*1 Thessalonians 5:16–18*

In writing to the believers in Thessalonica, Paul provided instructions for their daily spiritual lives. They were to make an effort to love one another and for their entire lives to be bathed in the love of Christ by rejoicing always, praying ceaselessly, and giving thanks in everything. These were key to the kind of spiritual life that was to define the Thessalonians—and us as well.

There are days when I simply don't want to rejoice, and I'm looking for any reason to be a grump! If I want an excuse, I can generally find one. However, on the other side of the scale, if I choose to rejoice, I generally can find a reason to be joyful as well. Therefore, we discover there is a choice involved when it comes to rejoicing because we can choose the lens with which we view the world.

Paul's second instruction—to pray without ceasing—has much to do with the first. How in the world can we really rejoice always? By praying without ceasing! Praying without ceasing is a mindset of continual communication with the Lord. It is living our ordinary lives completely and totally plugged in to intimacy with God. When we live in continuous communication with the Lord, then he is already present when we encounter difficult circumstances. Therefore, I can rejoice, for the Lord is the one who is there with me in the midst of challenges. Separation from God is the most desperate circumstance of life. Life lived in connection with God is the most joyful; therefore, in the midst of difficulty, we can rejoice because we are still connected to the Lord. But let's be honest, there are times when life changes at such a rapid pace that it's hard to keep up, let alone rejoice. The best thing we can do is stay connected to the one who can bring healing and comfort to the situation—by praying without ceasing.

Sometimes, in our desperate circumstances, we find that we want to run from the Lord and cling to our hurts. He invites us to bring our wounds to him, and then he helps us carry the pain. Remember that Jesus invited us to take on his yoke. Why? Because we're already carrying around a yoke of some kind, and when we try to carry it by ourselves, we will become completely weighed down. If we share the yoke with him, he takes the heavy part so that we can continue to move forward and to function. Pray. Pray without ceasing.

Finally, Paul instructed us to give thanks in everything. Really? In *everything*? This may seem like an exercise in futility, yet it is truly God's desire for each one of us to be able to be thankful in all circumstances. Does it come easily? I don't think so. The night that Jesus prayed in the garden of Gethsemane, he wasn't thankful that he was going to be crucified. He prayed that the Father would take the responsibility from him, if possible. At the same time, we can assume Jesus was grateful for the Father's presence and for his mission coming to completion. Jesus's burden wasn't easy, yet he persevered in prayer and went on to die on the cross, thereby saving all of humanity. Many who have suffered wonder whether there can really be a silver lining to their suffering. Paul knew that, if we only focused on the very worst part of our pain and suffering, we would never see Jesus. We are to look for the Lord, seek his face, pray without ceasing, and give thanks. Be careful—for suffering is not God's will, but we can find God's will in our response to suffering.

A few years ago, I gathered with a group of women in Wilmore, Kentucky, to pray for a dear follower of Jesus Christ who was extremely weak and suffering terribly from her cancer treatment. Those who knew this woman knew she was always looking for the silver lining, always seeking a way to rejoice. Although she was terribly ill, she had been sharing about her personal encounters with Jesus Christ and about how he continued to become more real to her on a daily basis. Through this suffering she had gotten to know him as never before. Those of us watching from the outside were astounded, for we had witnessed her deep and intimate relationship with Jesus for years, and it was hard to imagine there could be even more. I know that she did not feel like rejoicing every day and in every moment of her sickness, but she learned to see Jesus in her circumstances. No, life isn't easy, and we have no guarantee that things will always go well. Paul knew this, yet he encouraged Christ followers to rejoice, to pray, and to be thankful.

———◇———

And one thing more: Prepare a guest room for me, because I hope to be restored to you in answer to your prayers.

—*Philemon 1:22*

Paul sent a letter to a man named Philemon and asked him to restore his servant Onesimus. The situation was a bit tricky because Onesimus was a runaway slave who had become a believer. He was of great assistance to Paul and had become like a brother. This personal letter was written on behalf of Onesimus, but Paul felt comfortable reaching out to Philemon because Philemon had been praying for him. Paul made a connection between prayer and hospitality—because Philemon had prayed, Paul believed he could ask for a guest room to be prepared. This was a sign of hospitality but also of faith that God would answer Philemon's prayers. Paul mentioned that Philemon had been praying for his restoration. This would have been expected from another Christ follower. Those within the Christian community prayed for one another. They lifted up each other's needs and were willing to bear each other's burdens.

When we spend time in prayer for our sisters and brothers, their needs become our own needs. We are able to sense their burdens in new and palpable ways, and in doing so, we know better how to pray and also how to respond.

Paul himself had faith in his restoration because he believed in the power of prayer. Actually, he believed in the power of prayer because he believed in the one who answers prayer. Not only did Paul have faith, but the community of believers to whom he belonged also had faith. The faith of individuals was strengthened by the faith of the community.

Finally, the community of faith responded to needs through the practice of hospitality. Paul was able to ask them to have a guest room prepared. While we don't know for sure, one can imagine Philemon would have welcomed Paul into his home with open arms. The place would have been ready for him. Hospitality meant that those within the community of faith shared with each other and cared for one another's needs.

These are simple steps for those living within the community of faith. We are to take time to pray, lifting up our sisters and brothers in Christ. We pray for God to increase our faith to believe in and await restoration. The community of faith graciously greets one another with warm hospitality, for this is a reflection of life within the family of God.

Devotion to Prayer

1. Think about prayer becoming as important in your life as the air you breathe. What are ways in which you can pray continually?

   a. Practice praying before you get out of bed in the morning. Talk to the Lord about your upcoming day and ask for God's presence throughout.

   b. Practice praying before you eat every meal. Thank God for all that he has provided for you.

   c. Practice praying before you begin your day at work. Ask the Spirit to give you wisdom in all you do.

   d. Practice praying before you go to bed at night, thinking intentionally about where you noticed God's presence with you throughout the day, and thanking God for it, and asking for wisdom and direction for tomorrow.

2. Pray for opportunities to share the good news of Jesus Christ.

3. Pray for the Spirit to give you the words you need when the opportunity to share Christ arises.

4. Pray for your love to abound to those within the church community *and* to those outside. Look for

opportunities to minister to those who are not part of your church community.

5. Pray for those within your church community whom you know are facing difficult or challenging situations. Pray for opportunities to minister to their needs.

9

PRAGMATIC PRAYERS

———o———

I have told you these things, so that in me you may have peace. In this world you will have trouble. But take heart! I have overcome the world.

—John 16:33

Jesus had been telling his disciples the day would come when they would be confronted by those who would want to kill them. The religious zealots and others would be so deceived that they would believe they were serving God by persecuting and trying to murder Jesus's disciples. He wanted his disciples to be prepared for what they would face, for he knew they all would be put to death for their faith—except for John, who would live long enough to be an eyewitness to much of what would occur. Being a follower of Jesus Christ was not going to be easy, and it would include the adoption of a lifestyle that followed in the footsteps of the crucified Lord. Jesus's death on the cross brought about victory over sin and death and therefore provides peace. The world truly has been conquered through Jesus Christ, and for this we are eternally grateful. Today we pray for his peace in a world that is filled with trouble and persecution.

As I mull over this scripture, I am saddened by all that is happening and has happened in our world. We have witnessed the horrible persecution of different religious groups around the world, Christians included. We have witnessed unnecessary wars and all manner of political violence. In the middle of it all we find innocent people facing trouble of monumental proportions. It is overwhelming to even think about what some have had to suffer. Jesus's answer is no trite response to calamity, and it leaves us needing to explore what he is trying to say to us. Notice that he doesn't say he will end persecution to bring about peace. Instead, he says that we may find peace *in him*. Only in Christ can we can find real peace. This peace is found in a deep relationship with our Lord and Savior. It also means that, as Christ's followers, we are to pray for peace through him. We pray for those facing terrible death and persecution in various parts of the world, and we pray for a peace that comes from knowing and being in fellowship with Jesus Christ. He is the Prince of Peace and has come to bring us his peace.

The suffering that some people are facing in the world today is reprehensible. Knowing we can have peace in Christ is incredible, but we can't use that as an excuse to not become engaged in what is happening around us. While we pray that there are those who will sense the peace of Christ, we also take time for self-reflection and consider whether we are to be a voice for the marginalized and suffering. Is Christ asking us to take some responsibility for the suffering in our world? Pray for a response that comes from an obedient heart when nudged by the still, small voice of the Holy Spirit. The Lord may be asking us to speak up against injustice and take action. In our chaotic world, we pray that we will listen and obey the gentle voice that draws us toward the one who has conquered the world. Maybe, through prayer, we will be encouraged onward by the presence of the Spirit, challenging us to be silent no more.

———○———

Remember your leaders, who spoke the word of God to you. Consider the outcome of their way of life and imitate their faith.

—Hebrews 13:7

The letter to the Hebrews instructed readers to pray for those in leadership. These were the ones who had brought to them the word of God—without them they may not have known the way to salvation. The way that leaders chose to live their lives was important since the people were to look to them as examples and "imitate their faith." Why? Because they didn't yet have the complete Bible in the way we have it today. At that time, the letters were being circulated, but a church gathering would be grateful to have even one such letter. The main avenue for passing on the faith was through the witness of the everyday lives of the believers. No wonder they were in need of prayer!

Serving in a position of leadership has never been easy. Once someone steps into that role there will always be those who are unhappy with some of the things they do and decisions they make. There is simply no way for everyone to be happy all the time, but unfortunately we currently live in a culture that has cultivated the practice of being critical of leadership. The same may have been true in the early church, so we find these comments in the letter to the Hebrews useful. Our religious leaders have poured out their lives in service to God and the kingdom. We may not always agree with them, but they are dedicated servants of the Lord. We need to pray for them and be grateful for the ways they have led us to know the Lord. Their passion and desire to know Christ and to make a difference in the world should be imitated. Do they always do everything right? Probably not. Humans make mistakes. That is why they need prayer.

We should be challenged to imitate their faith. What would happen if imitating the faith of our religious leaders became our priority, rather than looking for ways to criticize them? We are not told in Scripture to criticize our leaders. We are told to pray for them. Oswald Chambers reminds us that God allows us to see the weaknesses in others not to criticize but so we can intercede. Thank God that you can see faults in our leaders—then use that knowledge as an opportunity to be engaged in prayer. God has revealed to you the area in which they need help, and this revelation can help focus your prayers.

Don't judge leadership for a single moment in which their best character may not have shone through. Instead, the letter to the Hebrews tells us we should "consider the outcome of their way of life." What does the whole story tell you? Look at the beauty of the entire portrait of one's life and the overall impact they have had as they have worked to faithfully serve in the kingdom. Recently my husband and I were in an art gallery. In one of the rooms, we came across a large Monet that had been painted later in the artist's life. When we looked at the painting up close, we couldn't see much, and we could have interpreted it as being of poor quality, saying it looked like a bunch of blobs of paint on a huge canvas. However, when we stepped back and looked at it from a distance, it was absolutely stunning. The big picture came together. It's easy to be critical when we are scrutinizing tiny details—but we may miss out on the beauty of the larger canvas. If we do not consider the entire life of a leader, we may get hung up on some small detail and miss the beauty of their life's portrait. Remember our leaders. Pray for them. Look at the big picture and imitate their faith so that God may use your life to paint the next masterpiece.

———o———

When I heard these things, I sat down and wept. For some days I mourned and fasted and prayed before the God of heaven.

"Lord, let your ear be attentive to the prayer of this your servant and to the prayer of your servants who delight in revering your name. Give your servant success today by granting him favor in the presence of this man."

—*Nehemiah 1:4, 11*

In the book of Nehemiah, we see Nehemiah himself become an example of the type of leader that God desires. In this opening chapter of the book, he heard the news of the situation in Jerusalem. He was overwhelmed with sorrow to hear of the conditions of his homeland. His heart was burdened, and he could not get away from the sense that God was asking him to respond. He became depressed as he grieved. For days he mourned and wept, but not only did he grieve, he also cried out to God. In his grief he did the hard work of praying, fasting, and pouring out his concerns before the Lord. He realized that only God could help him out of these circumstances, for who in their right mind could think they could bring about the reconstruction of the walls of Jerusalem?

While praying, Nehemiah became acutely aware of God's plan, and he began to pray into God's plan for success. This was not a human plan; he distinctly recognized God's desire. He didn't pray for the whole plan, just for the next step. He was going to have to broach the subject of helping Jerusalem with his boss, the king, to whom he was cupbearer. How would this go over? He didn't know, but he had to ask God to pave the way and for the king to have compassion on him. This was the first step in the completion of God's plan.

There are times when I feel that God speaks to me and genuinely gives me a plan for what he wants me to do. Sometimes I'm an impatient person, and I want to see the whole plan laid out before me from start to finish. I'd love to know the end game from the beginning. I also am typically better at *doing* than at *being*. I like to feel as if I'm getting in there and doing what God wants me to do. This can get me into trouble sometimes because I may take off and do things I think should be done without learning what God really wants from me. In my leadership role, I can learn a couple things from Nehemiah.

Great leaders take time to pray! In prayer, we are expected to *be* more than *do*. We are in a state of transformation. We recognize our weaknesses, place them before God, and learn to trust in him for guidance and direction. As we read through the Word of God, we discover that every great leader took time to go off alone and pray. They also fasted and prayed. They took prayer seriously because they realized that they could do nothing meaningful without the leadership of God in their lives. In our fast-paced world, taking time to pray may be viewed as wasteful. How in the world do we measure prayer? We don't—because it's not about doing but about being. Nehemiah spent an extended period of time in God's presence before he ever took action.

We too must learn to spend extended periods of time in God's holy presence before we jump into the business to which God has called us.

Great leaders take things one step at a time. While God may have given Nehemiah a vision for completing the reconstruction of the walls, Nehemiah also realized there needed to be a plan to get there. He would never be able to complete the reconstruction without the approval of the king. Therefore, he didn't spend time praying for the walls to be rebuilt. Instead, he prayed that God would speak to his boss and that his boss would be compassionate with him. This was the immediate need! There are times when we go to God in prayer and, instead of being sensitive to what we need to do in little chunks, we pray for the whole big picture. There is a time and place for praying for the big picture, but there is also a need to depend on God's leadership in the small steps that need to be taken to get to the big ones. Great leaders understand and follow God's leadership in the small things that must be accomplished in order to achieve the big picture. Those who only focus on the big picture tend to get frustrated when it doesn't come to fruition right away because they've not been willing to pay attention to the little things. Sometimes the little things seem insignificant, but a great leader is willing to invest time, energy, and prayer in the little things that become the building blocks to the big picture.

Prayer and seeking God's guidance in the little steps is where we need to begin. Neither of those two probably sounds very successful to the world's ears, but serving in the kingdom is not about being successful by human standards, and kingdom leadership begins by understanding this and by knowing that the principles we follow are not necessarily of this world.

Pragmatic Prayer

1. Pray for the persecuted church.

2. Pray for your leaders, even when you disagree with them.

3. Learn to seek God in your decision-making.
   a. Ask God to give you step-by-step guidance.

   b. Trust God for the next step.

   c. Pray that you are not anxious about what you do not yet understand.

10
PRAYER IN
THE PSALMS

———o———

As for me, I will be vindicated and will see your face; when I
awake, I will be satisfied with seeing your likeness.
—Psalm 17:15

In this psalm, David was wrestling with God in prayer. It physically consumed his body, and its culmination—after finishing the work of prayer—seemed to be that he was able to lie down to an exhausted sleep because he knew that the grace of God would come again and again. There isn't just one time of prayer, but there are continual seasons. When one season ends, another begins, and we are able to see that God comes over and over again. Together with the psalmist we can trust that we will be able to behold the face of our Savior. All of our tomorrows, no matter how difficult, are in

God's hands, and when the dawn breaks we will see the Lord face to face and know that this new day belongs to him.

I'm an achiever, and I like to tick things off my to-do list. The temptation is to embrace prayer in the same way, as something to finish and mark off my list, but if we view prayer that way it becomes perfunctory, obligatory, instead of what God wants, which is for it to be as natural as breathing. At the same time, there *is* effort involved in prayer, and sometimes we must work at it in persistent faith. The psalmist was troubled in many ways and had to pray through the physical nature of the spiritual battle, which meant that prayer became *work*. The idea of prayer being work may not sound pleasant, but we are facing battles that require us to put on our spiritual armor, and this is done through prayer, both individually and corporately. We need prayer meetings where we focus on the spiritual battles and the need for Christ to intercede for us with the Father. Our whole bodies participate in these prayers when we begin to see and experience what is happening in the spiritual realm. We cry out for our children and our grandchildren, asking for them to be protected from the evil one. We pray for intervention in the spiritual lives of our loved ones. We intercede for those who have wandered far from the faith.

I often pray in the night hours and then again in the early morning when I wake. There, the presence of God seems so real, and the Lord brings challenges to my own mind, encouraging me to pray about things that are new to my mind. Sometimes it's simply in the silence that God moves, and when I wake, I am satisfied, knowing I have beheld his likeness. Someday I will awake and see him clearly, face to face. That is also the promise of this psalm. In the resurrection we will be eternally satisfied and filled with joy as we behold our Savior's face. In the meantime, there are days that this journey feels like work, but we live in the promise that we will be satisfied.

———o———

May those who say to me, "Aha! Aha!" be appalled at their own shame. But may all who seek you rejoice and be glad in you; may those who long for your saving help always say, "The LORD is great!"

—Psalm 40:15–16

David the psalmist has taught us how to pray. The biblical record of his songs and prayers shows that he was a man who lived by the Spirit, following the leading of the Lord. He found himself in a situation where others mocked and shamed him. They looked at what he'd done and critically proclaimed, "Aha, aha! Look at what this man is doing and how ridiculous it looks!" He was brought to public discredit because of his faithfulness to God. The result was confusion and disgrace. David showed us that we are to pray against those who would publicly disgrace God's followers.

David moved on from praying against oppressors to praying for those who seek the Lord. Those who seek the Lord will find him and discover honor in knowing that the

Lord is far greater than the disgrace of the unbelievers who criticize. The love of God fills those who are saved, and instead of ridicule, they rejoice in their redemption, replying, "Great is the Lord!" Even the best followers of Jesus Christ will be undone if they do not live continually preserved by the grace of God.

It seems that society is standing at the ready to offer public criticism anytime it appears that a Christian has done something wrong. Because Jesus is our model for life and living, the challenge for the Christ follower can be great. The world has expectations of Christianity, and when we fail to meet those standards, there are plenty of folks ready to find fault and place blame. Certainly Christians should hold ourselves to a high standard, but we are human, and we will make mistakes, and sometimes we even succumb to temptation and sin. Although confession and repentance are important steps for all Christians to take following the commission of sin, the world is not always as willing to forgive us as God is. The world does not always believe that our confession and repentance are sincere, so sometimes when individual Christians sin or make public mistakes, the world chooses to blame and condemn all of Christianity.

David's guidance for us in responding to those who would come against Christianity? Pray for them! Ultimately, prayer can lead us to empathize with our detractors, understanding that those who say "Aha, aha!" will one day answer to God for their own actions—just as we all will. David's psalms are well known for turning even the darkest thoughts back toward God's glory, and this one is no different: those who seek the Lord will rejoice! God is in the business of transforming enemies into allies. Those who have been caught up in saying, "Aha, aha!" may eventually proclaim, "Great is the Lord!" We ought to follow David's lead in praying for those who come against us, that their eyes might be opened so that they can turn to God, and continually rejoice in the salvation found there. May the "Aha, aha!" be turned to godly praise. It is possible as we unite with our Father in prayer and lift up those who speak against us.

———o———

Pray for the peace of Jerusalem: "May those who love you be secure. May there be peace within your walls and security within your citadels." For the sake of my family and friends, I will say, "Peace be within you." For the sake of the house of the LORD our God, I will seek your prosperity.

—Psalm 122:6–9

The psalmist was writing and praying for his family and friends who were suffering in Jerusalem. He was interceding on their behalf and became very specific in his prayers. The city whose name meant "peace" was anything but peaceful. There was great need for peace and a sense of security. Their lives were in danger; therefore, he was willing to intercede on behalf of those he knew and loved. As God's children we are inextricably connected to one another; therefore, we pray for those who suffer for the sake of the house of the Lord our God. We seek the good, and we sacrifice for our sisters and brothers.

One evening I was overcome with sorrow as I watched the news reports on the suffering in Aleppo, Syria. Almost without a breath, the news reporter then went on to talk about U.S. politics. I was struck by the way he seemingly so easily shifted from one to the other. All of a sudden it felt like I was watching #FirstWorldProblems on the news in contrast to real problems. This psalm should convict us in regard to our lack of intercessory prayer on behalf of our brothers and sisters who are praying for peace to come to their city. The psalmist prayed for the peace of Jerusalem, for peace to come to God's people in that place, and we are called to intercede in prayer on behalf of those who are suffering as beloved children of the kingdom. Because of Christ, Christians in Aleppo—and everywhere—are our brothers and sisters, and we must pray for them as if we really know and believe that.

There are many people in our world who are suffering today. God's people are called to self-sacrificial service, honoring others above ourselves. Spending time in prayer is a gift of love that we joyfully give because of our participation with Jesus Christ and his mission to the world. There are brothers and sisters in Christ who will not be able to gather around a table to fellowship with family and friends, and they need us to pray for them and for peace and security to come within their walls.

———○———

How good and pleasant it is when God's people live together in unity! It is like precious oil poured on the head, running down on the beard, running down on Aaron's beard, down on the collar of his robe. It is as if the dew of Hermon were falling on Mount Zion. For there the LORD bestows his blessing, even life forevermore.

—Psalm 133

The unity found in the Trinity—the three-in-one—is to be reflected in God's people. Often we talk about the individual nature of our spiritual lives and growth with the resultant reflection of Christ in our lives. But corporately, as God's people, we are to grow ever closer to our Lord, being ever perfected and, in this case, reflecting the unity found in God. When this corporate reflection is visible, it spreads in a way that brings the healing balm of anointing oil to God's people and beyond. Unity among God's people is a vision of the end, of God's final purpose for humanity, as refreshing as the morning dew and a foreshadowing of the eternal. This future is anticipated in the coming of the Prince of Peace, and all the while, God's people are called to live into his unifying presence.

This psalm is one that can be both sung and prayed. We are called to pray for unity among God's people and, specifically, to pray for those who cause division. The enemy of our faith has no greater joy than to divide God's people. When we are fractured and overly critical of one another, there is no unity. The enemy works overtime on this project, for some of the worst fractures and divisions have occurred in the church.

Let us pray that God will unite God's children within the church, and across denominational lines, so that Christians will be the anointing balm this world needs. As long as we are fractured, we are unable to give witness to the Prince of Peace. Together, we can reflect the community of the holy Trinity, wrapped up in holy love, and shine God's light into the dark corners of our world.

———○———

Rescue me, Lord, from evildoers; protect me from the violent, who devise evil plans in their hearts and stir up war every day.

—Psalm 140:1–2

I call to you, Lord, come quickly to me; hear me when I call to you. May my prayer be set before you like incense; may the lifting up of my hands be like the evening sacrifice. Set a guard over my mouth, Lord; keep watch over the door of my lips.

—Psalm 141:1–3

David found himself in a difficult place, and Psalms 140 and 141 are filled with his angst over those who would accuse and speak evil of him. In the midst of his anguish, he poured out his heart to God. These psalms are filled with prayer because David recognized his need for prayer in this trial—and maybe not just the *place* of prayer but the *vocation* of prayer. He realized that prayer had to become part of his being and calling in life. Far too much of his life was beyond his control, and he was tempted to respond with his own words. Instead, we discover that his prayer included a request that the Lord would "keep watch over the door of my lips." His relationship with the Lord superseded anything else that was happening in his life, and he was determined that his life and prayers would continue to be an offering before the Lord.

David seemed to understand the serious nature of prayer. As a vocation, it became a part of his life and who he was. When we fail to take prayer seriously, it may reflect the fact that we do not understand the vocation of prayer: "The Christian vocation is to be in prayer, in the Spirit, at the place where the world is in pain, and as we embrace that vocation, we discover it to be the way of following Christ, shaped according to his messianic vocation to the cross, with arms outstretched, holding on simultaneously to the pain of the world and to the love of God."[1]

Oswald Chambers reminds us: "Prayer is *the* battle, and it makes no difference where you are. However God may engineer your circumstances, your duty is to pray. Never allow yourself this thought, 'I am of no use where I am,' because you certainly cannot be used where you have not yet been

---

1. N. T. Wright, *The Challenge of Jesus: Rediscovering Who Jesus Was and Is* (Downers Grove, IL: InterVarsity Press, 2015), 190.

placed. Wherever God has placed you and whatever your circumstances, you should pray, continually offering up prayers to him."[2]

When we get into the place of prayer with the Lord, we begin to experience the world through his perspective. "Learn new ways of praying with and from the pain, the brokenness, of that crucial part of the world where God has placed you. And out of that prayer discover the ways of being peacemakers, of taking the risk of hearing both sides, of running the risk of being shot at from both sides."[3] David knew what it was like to be shot at from both sides. Those for whom he fought eventually sought his demise. He became homeless, a man on the run with no place to lay his head, yet he called upon the Lord, desiring peace. He chose to live into the vocation of prayer while he guarded his mouth, and ultimately God intervened and was given the glory.

———o———

He will respond to the prayer of the destitute; he will not despise their plea. Let this be written for a future generation, that a people not yet created may praise the Lord.
—Psalm 102:17–18

The psalmist was well schooled in prayer. He had a deeply intimate relationship with God and knew he was

2. Oswald Chambers, *My Utmost for His Highest*, "October 17: The Key of the Greater Work," https://utmost.org/the-key-of-the-greater-work/.

3. Wright, *The Challenge of Jesus*, Kindle location 2539–41.

dependent on that relationship. God had answered his prayers in his times of deepest need. He would cry out when he was destitute, and God responded. God responded to his prayers not only for the here and now but also for future generations the psalmist himself would not see. However, the psalmist already had in his heart a desire for those who came after him to know the Lord as intimately as he did—so he prayed for his children and their children and their children, that they might all praise the Lord!

We may be able to identify many reasons to pray, but they all spring out of the intimacy found in prayer. The Lord hears the prayers of the destitute! Maybe this is a foreshadowing of the Sermon on the Mount, where we are told, "Blessed are the poor in spirit" (Matthew 5:3)—because, once we realize that all that we have is nothing compared to the Lord, then we are destitute, and we realize we are poor in spirit. The result is a prayer life that is consumed with a desire to be near to him. The number-one reason to pray is to know Christ! We will never get to know him the way he desires if we don't make it a priority to spend time with him in order to get to know him and allow him to mold us and shape us into a reflection of his image. Without knowing Christ everything else is worthless. All of our actions and responses are to come from a deep and passionate relationship with Jesus Christ. Only when we get to know the heart of Christ will our hearts break for the things that break his heart—and then we will know how to pray for others. We will wake in the middle of the night and have such an overwhelming burden for someone that all we can do is join with Christ in prayer for that individual. We will be sitting in a church service when, all of a sudden, we will know that a particular person is struggling, and we will join in prayer with Christ for them.

We recognize the spiritual battle because we sense it through our intimacy with Christ. This intimacy with Christ draws us deeper into our walk with him—so deep that it becomes sweet and beautiful. There are moments when you feel you can almost touch him, and you pray that everyone could have this experience. This is when we begin to cry out in prayer for our loved ones, desiring them to know the deep, deep love of Jesus. You pray for your children and your nieces and nephews, and you pray for future in-laws you don't even know yet, and you pray for grandchildren who aren't even born yet, and you pray for great-grandchildren whom you may never see—yet you pray! We pray because we are desperately in love with Jesus, and we want people "not yet created" to praise the Lord!

Why pray? Because, without prayer, there will be no spiritual life—indeed, no *life*. I think this is one reason my grandfather gave of himself in prayer. His prayers, prayed so long ago, continue to impact my life, my children's lives, even my grandchildren, and someday my great-grandchildren. We pray so future generations will have life abundant.

Praying with the Psalmist

1. Prepare yourself for times when prayer will be work. What might be the obstacles to that work, and how can you work through those obstacles?

2. Pray for those who actively come against you or Christianity.

3. As you read or watch the news, pray for those who are suffering. Pray for peace to come to the places of the world where there is strife.

4. Pray that God would keep watch over the door of your lips.

5. Pray that prayer might become your vocation in life.

6. Pray for the next generation, and the next, and the next.

CLOSING THOUGHTS

I was hesitant to write this simple book on prayer, for there is still so much I need to learn about spending time in God's presence. It seems that once you begin to get to know God, you discover there is still much more to know. In that space you begin to realize how little you really understand because of the incredible greatness of our God. I'm a servant on a journey, wanting to know more of Christ.

Along my journey there have been those who have been superb examples and mentors in prayer. Great women like Aletha Hinthorn, Cheryl Roland, Joy Wisehart, and Patsy Lewis have impacted me beyond anything I would have imagined. Their continued prayerful mentorship and guidance encourages me on my spiritual pilgrimage. They are a reminder that we do not travel alone but within and along the community of faith.

My prayer is that God might use this book to help someone draw closer to the Lord. In this day and age, we need a renewed emphasis on prayer, and we need people who will be willing to sacrifice their time and energy interceding for others and praying for spiritual revival. If you've read this far, then I pray you will be one of those who will enter into a deeper walk with Christ, ever in awe of the greatness of God, and that God will use you to help transform our world.